Sixth Edition

D0217329

The Actor in You

Twelve Simple Steps to Understanding the Art of Acting

Robert Benedetti

Boston   Columbus   Indianapolis   New York   San Francisco   Upper Saddle River
Amsterdam Cape Town   Dubai   London   Madrid Milan   Munich   Paris   Montréal   Toronto
Delhi Mexico City   São Paulo   Sydney   Hong Kong   Seoul   Singapore   Taipei   Tokyo

This book is dedicated to the memory of a great actress, my first love and lifelong friend, Karen Black.

Editor in Chief: Ashley Dodge
Senior Acquisitions Editor: Melissa Mashburn
Editorial Assistant: Courtney Turcotte
Director of Marketing: Brandy Dawson
Executive Marketing Manager: Kelly May
Senior Marketing Coordinator: Theresa Rotondo
Managing Editor: Denise Forlow
Program Manager: Maggie Brobeck
Project Manager: Rebecca Sage/Integra Software Services, Ltd
Senior Operations Supervisor: Mary Fischer
Operations Specialist: Mary Ann Gloriande
Art Director: Jayne Conte

Cover Designer: Suzanne Behnke
Cover Image: Robert Benedetti
Director of Digital Media: Brian Hyland
Digital Media Project Management: Learning Mate Solutions, Ltd.
Digital Media Project Manager: Tina Gagliostro
Full-Service Project Management and Composition: Integra Software Services Pvt. Ltd.
Printer/Binder: Courier
Cover Printer: Courier
Text Font: 10/12, Sabon LT Std

Cover Image: Cover photo of Barbara Tarbuck as Anna in the author's production of Brecht's Mother Courage at the Nevada Conservatory Theatre, 2007. Photo by the author.

Credits and acknowledgments borrowed from other sources and reproduced, with permission, in this textbook appear on appropriate page within the text.

Library of Congress Cataloging-in-Publication Data
Benedetti, Robert L.
  The actor in you : twelve simple steps to understanding the art of acting / Robert Benedetti. — 6th edition.
    pages cm
    Includes index.
    ISBN-13: 978-0-205-91490-6
    ISBN-10: 0-205-91490-X
  1. Acting. I. Title.
PN2061.B392 2015
792.02'8—dc23

2013043051

10 9 8 7 6 5 4 3 2 1

ISBN-10: 0-205-91490-X
ISBN-13: 978-0-205-91490-6

CONTENTS

PART TWO   ACTION AND CHARACTER

PREFACE

My book for advanced actors, *The Actor at Work*, has been through ten editions over more than forty years in print. When I first set out to write this book for beginning actors I had to examine the advanced book and distill from it the most fundamental elements of the art, find a way to express them in simple language, and arrange them in a logical and effective sequence. This process was a valuable experience for me, and over the five subsequent editions I have had a chance to refine my own understanding of the art of acting as I received comments from users and the reviewers of the first five editions. Most useful was my own recent experience in teaching beginning acting; I was surprised at the changes in students over the past several years as the impact of the digital revolution revealed itself in their changing relationship to the text and the act of speaking aloud. As a result, I have revised *The Actor in You* extensively.

New to the Sixth Edition

This book is designed for students at the introductory level, whether they are beginning a training process to become professional actors or merely want to enhance their understanding and appreciation of the actor's art; the language has been kept simple and direct, and terminology is carefully explained when introduced.

- This sixth edition has been revised according to many suggestions from users of the previous editions and input from my students and professional actors who have used the book.
- This edition has been reorganized from the original sixteen steps into twelve easy steps that lead to an understanding and experience of the acting process.
- The overall structure has been simplified from four parts to three. This tightening of the book's structure is intended to give instructors more latitude to vary the content of the course to fit their own teaching approaches.
- A new chapter has been added on voice and speech in recognition of the fact that today's students, children of the digital revolution, have less experience in speaking aloud than did previous generations.
- Yet another new chapter provides the basis for an initial analysis of the text.
- Another new chapter has been added on personalization with techniques for entering into the life of the character.
- The final steps now provide a more complete view of the rehearsal process.
- Throughout, I use examples from three widely available plays: Arthur Miller's *Death of a Salesman*, Lorraine Hansberry's *A Raisin in the Sun*, and Tennessee Williams's *The Glass Menagerie*. These plays should be read at the outset in order to better understand my examples.

This text is available in a variety of formats—digital and print. To learn more about Pearson's titles, pricing options and customization opportunities, visit www.pearsonhighered.com.

Glossary

Many theater terms are defined in the glossary at the end of the book. These terms are in **boldface** when they first appear in the body of the text.

Teaching Guide

The author has written a Teaching Guide (0-205-91493-4) to accompany *The Actor in You: Twelve Simple Steps to Understanding the Art of Acting*. This supplement is available as a downloadable file at www.pearsonhighered.com/irc (access code required).

Acknowledgments

My thanks to the many students and colleagues who have contributed to my understanding of the acting process, either by their teaching or by their artistry. Thanks also to those who reviewed the manuscript for this edition: Sheldon Deckelbaum, San Diego Mesa College; Richard Poole, Briar Cliff University; Wendy Wisely, Santa Rosa Junior College.

About the Author

A distinguished teacher of acting and directing, and recipient of multiple Emmy and Peabody Awards as a film producer, Robert Benedetti received his Ph.D. from Northwestern University. He was an early member of Chicago's Second City Theatre and then taught acting for over fifty years at schools including the University of Wisconsin–Milwaukee, Carnegie Mellon University, the National Theatre School of Canada, the University of California–Riverside, the University of Nevada–Las Vegas, and the Santa Fe University of Art and Design. He was Chairman of the Programme in Theatre at York University in Toronto, Chairman of the acting program at the Yale Drama School, and Dean of Theatre at the California Institute of the Arts.

Dr. Benedetti has directed at many regional theaters—including the Tyrone Guthrie Theatre; the Oregon, Colorado, and Great Lakes Shakespeare festivals; and the Milwaukee, San Diego, and South Coast Repertory Theatres—and overseas at the Melbourne Repertory Theatre (Australia), Repertory Theatre and the Berlin Festival.

As a film writer and producer, he won three Emmys and a Peabody award for producing *Miss Evers' Boys* and *A Lesson before Dying* for HBO. He has written and produced numerous other films.

In 2005, Benedetti received the Lifetime Career Achievement Award from the Association for Theatre in Higher Education. In 2012, he was inducted into the College of Fellows of the American Theatre.

Dr. Benedetti has written six books on acting and film production, including *The Actor at Work (Tenth Edition)*, *ACTION! Acting for Film and Television*, and *From Concept to Screen: An Overview of Film and Television Production*. All are available from Pearson Education.

PART ONE

Preparing Yourself

Buddhists describe the process of personal growth as the "threefold way." It begins with preparing the *ground*, in the way a gardener cultivates the soil to make it ready to accept the seed. Next a *path* is opened, as when the gardener plants the seed and waters the young plant. Finally, the *fruition* follows naturally, as when the gardener perfects the plant by pruning and tending, always with respect for its own nature.

We will use this idea of the threefold way of ground, path, and fruition to organize our study of acting. Part 1 of this book will begin with you, your body, your voice, and your sense of purpose as an actor. You are the "ground," the instrument, of your work as an actor.

Part 2 will open the "path" you can travel on your way to becoming an actor. This is the concept of *action*, the living experience of entering your character's world and mind. Here we will explore your ability to experience the needs and thoughts of the character within his or her circumstances, and to experience for yourself the things the character says and does to try to satisfy those needs. From this experience will come a natural transformation as you begin to personalize the character, to discover that new version of yourself which will become the character. The great Russian director Stanislavski once said that every performance is a marriage of actor and character; Part 2 will establish the foundations of that marriage and the techniques whereby it can be achieved.

The "fruition" of this process, the performance and after, will make up Part 3 of the book. Here you will consider the conduct of rehearsals and the staging of the show. Building on what you discovered in Part 2, you will develop an artistically heightened creation that serves the purposes intended by the author within the demands of the staging chosen by your director and designers.

There are exercises in each lesson in this book. They are a program of self-discovery and self-development and are arranged roughly according to a "natural" acquisition of skills and insights. The experiences provided by the exercises are essential to a true understanding (in the muscles as well as in the mind) of what this book is about. These exercises have no "right" outcome, so just follow the instructions and see what happens.

Why Study Acting?

There are many reasons to study acting. You may be considering a professional acting career; you may think the study of acting will help you present yourself more effectively in everyday life; or you may simply wish to increase your enjoyment of plays, films, and TV shows. Whatever your reason, you will discover that the study of acting can also be a process of self-exploration that can expand your spiritual, psychological, and physical potential. Brian Bates, a psychologist who also teaches acting, lists some of the ways in which the study of acting can contribute to personal growth:

> Finding our inner identity. Changing ourselves. Realizing and integrating our life experience. Seeing life freshly and with insight into others. Becoming aware of the powers of our mind. Risking and commitment. Learning how to concentrate our lives into the present, and the secrets of presence and charisma. Extending our sense of who we are, and achieving liberation from restricted concepts of what a person is.[1]

Even if the study of acting serves no immediate personal purpose, it can give you an enhanced understanding of real-life behavior, especially the way people behave in pursuit of their needs and desires. Drama is the one art that is entirely concerned with the way people think, feel, and interact with one another and with their world. Great plays from all times, places, and cultures reveal to us the underlying patterns and truths of the human condition, including our own.

In all these ways, the study of acting, even if it does not lead to a professional career, is a meaningful journey of personal discovery and self-expansion. Through acting you can explore your own thoughts and feelings, have experiences far beyond what your real life offers you, live in new worlds, and say and do things you would never be able to experience otherwise. What a wonderful adventure!

---

[1]Brian Bates, *The Way of the Actor* (Boston: Shambhala, 1987), p. 7.

STEP 1

Understanding
the Actor's Job

LEARNING OBJECTIVES

- Distinguish the qualities that produce an effective performance in any medium: audience engagement and attention; truthfulness and believability; the fulfillment of dramatic function.

In the simplest sense, an actor is anyone who performs a role in a play, TV show, or movie. Each of these three media—stage, small screen, and big screen—requires its own techniques, skills, and approaches, and few actors are equally good at all of them. A good TV sitcom actor, for instance, may not do well in a dramatic feature film, while an accomplished feature film actor may fail to deliver a stageworthy performance in a live theater. Moreover, the many different kinds of material performed in each medium, from hilarious comedy to heartbreaking tragedy, make different emotional and technical demands on actors, and again, not every actor is good at all of them. An accomplished comic actor, for instance, may not do well in a serious role, and vice versa.

Regardless of the medium and type of material, however, there are certain basic things that *all* good actors in all media and with all types of material must be able to do. These fundamental skills, specifically those required by the live theater, will be the aim of our study in this book, as step-by-step we lay a foundation on which future work may be based.

The most common perception of the actor's job is that he or she creates a *character*. A good actor does this with a completeness and intensity that not only embodies the character but also invites us to experience the character directly through our participation in the character's behavior and the thoughts behind that behavior. Thus the creation of an effective characterization involves not only physical and vocal aspects but also thoughts, emotions, values, beliefs, needs, and all the qualities that distinguish a complete and unique personality.

Moreover, the character is created not only to express the truth of human behavior and personality but also to fulfill the purpose for which the character

3

was created in the telling of the play's story. A character never lives unto himself or herself, separate from the story of which he or she is a functioning part, and the good actor is never concerned with the creation of a character that stands apart from the world of the play and the function of the character within that world. In this sense, the actor is a kind of *storyteller*.

Having said that an actor's job is fundamentally the creation of a characterization that serves the demands of the story being told, with all the thoughts and emotions required to render the characterization complete and believable, let's look at other, deeper qualities that distinguish good acting.

Engagement

Every good actor strives to create a performance that is *engaging*, that draws the spectators in, invites them to participate in the life of the character, and compels their attention in whatever way is required by the material. This engagement is what makes all the other components of the actor's work—emotion, character, and storytelling—possible. Let's begin, then, by considering what makes a performance engaging.

In 350 BCE, Aristotle became the first Western philosopher to describe the qualities of a good play, and one of the qualities he believed to be necessary was *sympatheia*, or "fellow-feeling," the ability of the audience to recognize the characters as fellow human beings. This is what we commonly call "believability." Notice, however, that believability is relative to the style, content, and intent of the material being performed. Naturalistic plays, fantasies, slapstick comedies, classical tragedies, sitcoms, political satires, and the wide range of other performance forms all create their own worlds, each with its own sense of believability, some far removed from the appearances of everyday life. In all media and types of material, it is the world of the story that establishes what is "real," and the actor's performance must be believable and therefore engaging within that world.

Whatever the demands of the specific material, an engaging performance always connects with us in a personal way; it draws us in and makes us feel as if we are "in" the characters and their world. This sense of engagement on a personal level is called *empathy*, which literally means "in-feeling." Empathy is not the same as sympathy; we can feel "in" a character even if the character is unsympathetic (indeed, some of the most vivid characters in the history of drama are villains). Given a good performance by the actor, we can empathize with a character even if his or her values, behavior, and world are very different, even contrary, to our own.

This, in fact, is one of the great values of the dramatic experience: We can learn much about ourselves by feeling what it is like to do things, hold values, and live in worlds that are foreign to us. A leading American director likened doing a play to an archeological dig, since the acting and directing processes enable both makers and spectators to venture into different times, places, values, and behaviors and experience them firsthand. This is especially true of older plays and plays from other cultures, but even a contemporary play can offer new insights into our own world and behavior, helping us to see our familiar world in new ways.

In fact, most actors especially enjoy playing roles that require them to reach out into new experiences and to explore new, dormant, or hidden aspects of themselves. One of the greatest rewards of being an actor is this unending opportunity for self-discovery and self-expansion. The actor is, in a way, an explorer of the human psyche and condition; he or she journeys into the life of the character and the character's world and then reports back to us by embodying the essence of what has been discovered, expressed in a heightened and purified form.

When the actor accomplishes this, the spectator is invited to go along on the journey of exploration and become personally engaged, experiencing the character and the character's world and the events that occur there "as if they are before our eyes," as Aristotle put it. This **immediacy**, he felt, was the essential quality of great drama and distinguished it from all other forms of literature and performance. A great play well performed is not *about* an event; it *is* the living event itself "as if before our eyes." For this reason we will, in the first steps, emphasize the need for the actor to work in the here and now. The immediacy of the dramatic performance is potentially memorable and life changing; at its best, theater creates something truthful that will enrich and perhaps even change the audience's lives. This is the ultimate result of engagement.

Truthfulness

Aristotle wondered why we eagerly watch a play that presents a painful spectacle, such as the tragedy *Oedipus Rex*, in which a man discovers that he has unknowingly murdered his father and then married his mother. How can such an awful experience attract us? Aristotle's answer was that we can enjoy a painful play because we learn something truthful from it, and learning the truth, Aristotle believed, is "our greatest joy." Therefore, we can say that the best kind of actor *engages the audience in order to communicate truth*. Even material meant to be a pleasant escape, such as a TV sitcom, is more valuable and enjoyable if it offers some measure of truthfulness and insight. Indeed, the greatest sitcoms—such as *M.A.S.H., Cheers, Seinfeld, Modern Family, Will & Grace, The Office, 30 Rock*, and others—all contained some measure of truth. One in particular, *All in the Family*, with its character of Archie Bunker, made real changes in American society by using humor to defuse serious issues like racial prejudice.

It is difficult to express precisely what we mean by the idea of "truth" in art, perhaps hardest of all in theater, film, and television, which function as both commerce and art. The commercial demands of the media are often at odds with the desire to present truth, and much commercially successful entertainment contains no truth at all—some even reinforces false and destructive stereotypes. It is left to the ethical commitment and skill of each artist to ensure that truth somehow survives commercial pressures. We often speak of the actor's physical and vocal skills as his or her **craft**, and it is interesting that the word "craft" comes from the German word for "power." Through his or her skill, the actor has the potential power to affect the lives of the spectators, and it is the ethical responsibility of the good actor to use this power for a meaningful and truthful purpose. Like the doctor, the actor should "first do no harm."

It is easier to say what theatrical truth is *not*: It is not an obsequious appeal for the audience's favor at any cost; it is not the reinforcement of stereotypes that deny the uniqueness of individual human beings; it is not propaganda that distorts reality in favor of a particular point of view; it is not mere impersonation that mimics the appearances of everyday life, however believable that may be, without expressing some deeper insight; it is not the creation of an emotional state for its own sake, no matter how moving it may be; it is not an actor's selfish display that distracts from one's fellow actors or the meaning of the story.

Truth is a personal matter driven by the life experience of each artist, and part of a serious professional actor's job is to discover what he or she recognizes as truthful in a performance and what he or she has to say about the human condition through that performance. The work of all the great theater makers throughout history has been based on their search for truth, and their techniques were attempts to find the best ways to express that truth: The naturalism of Stanislavski, the presentationalism of Meyerhold, the demonstrative epic style of Brecht, the heightened physicality of Grotowski, the use of non-Western masks and puppets by Julie Taymor, and the many other ways of making theater were all an effort to find and express theatrical truth.

Skill

When Aristotle wondered how we can enjoy watching a painful tragedy, he said that besides the truth the experience offers, we can also enjoy the *skill* of the performer. The qualities that attract us to great actors are the same things that make us appreciate great athletes: their seemingly effortless skill, their total concentration on the job at hand, and their tremendous sense of aliveness. Notice that like the great athlete, the actor's skill should never draw attention to itself in the sense of "grand standing" or trying to get the audience's attention in inappropriate ways. We marvel at the "artlessness," the transparency of the actor who can transport us completely into the world of the story and make us forget that we are watching a rehearsed performance. Actors who are able to work in this way become compelling; we sometimes say that we "can't take our eyes off them."

In a basic way, actors do things we all do: They speak, move, and have thoughts and emotions. What makes actors special is not so much *what* they do, but the special *way* in which they do it. You already have many of the basic skills you need to be an actor; what you need to learn are the actor's special ways of using those skills in a *heightened* and *purified* way. A sociologist noticed this fact fifty years ago, when he said:

> It does take deep skill, long training, and psychological capacity to become a good stage actor. But...almost anyone can quickly learn a script well enough to give a charitable audience some sense of realness.... Scripts even in the hands of unpracticed players can come to life because life itself is a dramatically enacted thing.... In short, we all act better than we know how.[2]

---

[2]Erving Goffman, *The Presentation of Self in Everyday Life* (New York: Doubleday, 1959), pp. 71–74. Copyright © by Erving Goffman.

Nonetheless, performing for the stage or camera requires that these everyday abilities be heightened, purified, and brought within the control of a purposeful discipline. As the psychologist and acting teacher Brian Bates, whom we quoted earlier, put it:

> Almost everything that actors do can be identified with things we do in less dramatic form in everyday life. But in order to express the concentrated truths which are the life-stuff of drama, and to project convincing performances before large audiences, and the piercing eye of the film and television camera, the actor must develop depths of self-knowledge and powers of expression far beyond those with which most of us are familiar.[3]

This book will help you begin to develop your everyday acting skills into the greater power of artistic technique. Your job is to recognize, focus, and strengthen the natural actor you already are. Only you can do this, but the ideas and exercises in this book provide insights and experiences to help you fulfill and develop your natural talents.

Usefulness

All the various approaches to theater and acting throughout our history have tried to communicate experiences that would relate directly to the lives of the spectators in a meaningful way. The great Russian director Stanislavski, the source of much of our modern theater practice, put it this way early in the twentieth century:

> You must love your chosen profession because it gives you the opportunity to communicate ideas that are important and necessary to your audience...to educate your audience and to make them better, finer, wiser, and more useful members of society.[4]

A good actor, then, strives to create a performance that is not only engaging and truthful but also relevant and useful to the lives of the spectators and thereby to the world, within the demands of the particular material being performed.

There is one way that all great acting can be relevant to our lives. Although a play may teach us something about who we are, the actor's ability to be transformed teaches us something about who we may *become*. Watching an actor creating a new personal reality, a new self, can remind us that we, too, have that same capacity for self-definition and that change and personal growth is possible even in difficult circumstances. In this way, our theater can again be a celebration of our personal potential and of the ongoing flow of life, just as it was in its beginnings in ancient Greece as an offering to Dionysus, the god of transformation and the life force. An actor who works in this spirit finds his

---

[3]Bates, *The Way of the Actor.*

[4]Quoted by Nikolai Gorchakov in *Stanislavski Directs* (New York: Funk & Wagnalls, 1954), p. 40.

or her horizons being continually broadened by a sense of ethical and spiritual purpose.

Dramatic Function

It is not enough for an actor to be engaging, truthful, skillful, and useful. As we said earlier, a good performance must also contribute to the particular story being told. Every character in a play has been created by the writer to do a certain job within the world of that play. There are many things characters may be created to do: They may move the plot forward, provide an obstacle to some other character, provide information, represent some value or idea, provide comic relief, and so on. Whatever the character was created to do, the actor must above all else create a performance that successfully does that particular job. We will call this the **dramatic function** of the role. Fulfilling this dramatic function is the most important responsibility of a good actor.

To sum up, all good actors strive to fulfill the dramatic function of their role in an engaging, truthful, and skillful way that is relevant and useful to the lives of the spectators within the demands of the particular performance. That's a tall order to be sure, and not even the best actors achieve it in every performance, but these are the qualities that all good actors strive for in their work.

EXERCISE 1.1: WRITING A REVIEW

Pick a performance you have seen recently in the theater; if you have not had such an experience, you may select a film or TV performance; in any case, it should be a performance that made a strong impression on you. Write a review of the performance that examines the qualities discussed thus far.

1. In what ways was the actor *engaging*?
2. Did you feel yourself to be *in the character's place* and in his or her world?
3. Was the performance *skillful* without calling attention to itself?
4. Was it *truthful* within the world and manner of the story?
5. Did it serve the *dramatic function* of the character within the story?
6. What did you learn about your own life or your own world from this performance?
7. How was it useful to you?

Finding Your Own Sense of Purpose

For those who have made acting not just a career but a way of life (and this includes all our greatest actors), it is clear that acting addresses needs and motivations far deeper than the desire for attention or material success. There can be many such personal needs; some actors speak of the release that playing a role gives them, from what Alec Guinness called "my dreary old life"; for them, acting gives them permission to have experiences they would never dare have in real life. Patrick Stewart, best known as Captain Picard on *Star Trek* and who is also a great Shakespearean actor, once told me: "What first attracted me to acting was the fantasy world of the theater into which I could escape from the much less pleasant world of my childhood." For others, acting may provide compensation for a sense of personal unworthiness, allowing them to receive attention and approval within the guise of the roles they play. Yet others are driven to act by some ethical, political, or social passion, using their art to help change society in some beneficial way. Whatever the motivation may be, those with such deep sources of energy often have the best chance for a professional life; the life of an actor is difficult at best, and only very deep motivations can sustain a career.

It will be useful for you to discover if you have any such needs or desires that can help to motivate and sustain you in your study; even if you do not intend an acting career, identifying some deeper purpose can enhance your learning process and make you a more effective student. Begin by doing this simple exercise.

EXERCISE 1.2: GOING BACK TO THE BEGINNING

Relax and close your eyes. Let yourself travel back in your memories to the earliest experience you can remember of an acting performance that made an impression on you.

1. Where were you?
2. How old were you?
3. Who were with you?
4. What was it about the performance that struck you?
5. How did it make you feel?
6. As you relive this experience, are there even earlier memories of any kind that come up?
7. Thinking back to this experience, is there anything about it that eventually brought you to the study of acting?
8. Can you see in this experience anything that you might want from acting, or something you might want to achieve through acting?

A sense of purpose can be a powerful source of energy and commitment, especially if it is something you care about deeply, something that is bigger and more important to you than your own success. It may take many forms: It may be psychological or personal, such as wanting a sense of belonging, or a chance to express yourself in a way you can't in everyday life, or a chance to feel worthy of attention and even love. Or, it may be ethical or political, such as a love of justice; a hatred of bigotry; a desire for a more kind, peaceful, and loving world. It may even be religious in nature. Whatever it may be, recognizing it can help guide you toward the kind of theater that will be most satisfying for you and in which you are likely to be most effective because you are working from your deepest energy source. This spirit of service will overcome self-consciousness and carry you beyond yourself, giving you a transcendent purpose from which will come strength, courage, dignity, fulfillment, and ongoing artistic vitality.

EXERCISE 1.3: YOUR MANIFESTO

A manifesto is a written public declaration of belief and intention. In politics there have been many famous manifestos, such as our own Declaration of Independence; in art, there have been manifestos declared by many movements, such as the Dadaists and the Surrealists. What all manifestos have in common is that they lay out a set of goals and indicate the means whereby those goals may be reached.

1. Write your own manifesto as an actor. Give considerable thought to what you might want to achieve through your acting, and therefore the kind of actor you intend to become. Express this as a short (less than one page), strongly felt written statement.
2. Stand up in front of your group and read your manifesto with full conviction. Make it a strong and memorable statement. Drive it home to your listeners.

Discipline

Finally, we must consider the quality that is most necessary to an actor's long-term growth and development in mastering the art of acting—*discipline.*

Real discipline is not a matter of following someone else's rules. In the best sense, it is your acceptance of responsibility for your own development through systematic effort. You accept this responsibility not to please someone else, not to earn a grade or a good review or a job, but because you choose to become all that you can be.

Discipline is rooted in your *respect* for yourself, as well as your respect for your fellow workers, for your work, and for the world you serve through that work. Poor discipline is really a way of saying, "I'm not worth it" or "What I do doesn't matter." Discipline will come naturally if you can acknowledge your own value, the importance and seriousness of your work, and the great need for your work in the world.

Discipline requires *regularity.* Your work, especially on technical skills of body and voice, must be a prolonged and systematic effort. Stanislavski, looking back late in his life, had this to say:

> Let someone explain to me why the violinist who plays in an orchestra on the tenth violin must daily perform hour-long exercises or lose his power to play? Why does the dancer work daily over every muscle in his body?...And why may the dramatic artist do nothing, spend his day in coffee houses and hope for the gift [of inspiration] in the evening?[5]

---

[5]Constantin Stanislavski, *My Life in Art,* trans. J. J. Robbins (New York: Theatre Arts Books, 1952). Copyright © 1924 by Little, Brown & Co. and 1952 by Elizabeth Reynolds Hapgood.

Working steadily and for the long term, with patience and a sense of striving together, with our fellow theater artists, and being willing to risk the momentary failure for the sake of the long-term success—these are the attitudes you must nurture. The pressures of our educational system and of performance itself work against these attitudes, as does the normal desire we all have to succeed. Resist these pressures. As a student, you are in the unique position of working in a relatively safe environment, one in which you are encouraged to take risks and to stretch yourself beyond your established limits. Hopefully, you will be supported even in failure if that failure results from an honest effort to expand and perfect your skills. Enjoy your freedom as a student to explore a variety of approaches and experiences; enjoy the journey, the exploration itself.

Summary of Step 1

All good actors strive to create characters that fulfill the dramatic function for which they were created, and they strive to do so in an engaging, truthful, and skillful way in order to provide experiences that are relevant and useful to the spectator and the world. They are often driven and sustained in their work by deeply felt needs and desires of a personal, social, or political kind, and from their sense of purpose comes courage and tenacity. The work of the actor also requires discipline, which is rooted in respect for self and seriousness of purpose, and the acceptance of responsibility for personal development through systematic effort.

Note: For a brief history of acting, see Appendix A.

STEP 2

Relaxing and Centering

LEARNING OBJECTIVES

- Experience centered relaxation in the form most useful to the actor, with special emphasis on the breath.
- Explore from this centered position the flow of bodily and vocal energy as you begin to move and sound on stage, and also experience also the effect of gravity on your movements and bodily alignment.

Acting requires that all aspects of your being—your body, voice, thoughts, and feelings—be available, integrated, and controllable. They are the tools of your trade. You also need a capacity for fantasy and playfulness, and all these qualities are native to you: As a child, you began life in a state of wholeness and openness, with a natural ability for engaging in fantasy and for playing with others. In the process of growing up, you may have begun to lose some of that natural wholeness and openness. There may be some aspects of your body and voice, some forms of expression, some feelings, thoughts, and experiences that you have learned to ignore or suppress. For example, physical touching and being touched in public may be uncomfortable for you at first. Several of the exercises that follow will require physical contact between you and your fellow students, and if this is uncomfortable for you, share your concern privately with your teacher. Then, if you wish, you can—with your teacher's support—use your exploration of the acting process to begin overcoming physical shyness and to become more confident and comfortable in your physical identity.

You can recapture the childlike qualities of wholeness, openness, and imaginativeness best when you are relaxed, playful, and nonjudgmental. Some psychologists call this the **creative state**, which is produced when your "internal parent" allows your "inner child" to come out and play. The first and most important step toward this creative state is **relaxation**, which naturally leads to greater openness and responsiveness. In a relaxed state, you will find it easy to experience what we call **centeredness**, to begin moving and sounding in a more fully integrated and controllable way, and to enter into a more free and open exchange of energy with your fellow workers. These three qualities—relaxation, centeredness, and openness to others—are the foundation of what is, for the professional actor, the work of a lifetime of physical, vocal, mental, and spiritual development.

Relaxation

For most of us, performing arouses anxiety. This can be both pleasurable (as in the excitement of creative discovery) and unpleasant (as in the fear of failure). In either case, anxiety can make your muscles tense and disrupt your breathing and thinking, "freezing" you and interfering with your ability to react and to explore playfully. Tension is the greatest enemy of the creative state, and for some **stage fright** can become so acute as to be debilitating; the great British actor Sir Laurence Olivier suffered from it so badly at one point in his career that he had to stop acting for a time.

When you find yourself stiff with anxiety, you may attempt to compensate by trying harder, by putting more effort into your work and trying to force your way through it. Unfortunately, this is exactly the wrong thing to do. Excessive effort only increases your tension and further reduces your freedom of creative response. Think, for example, of trying to open a drawer that is stuck: If you tug at it with all your might, chances are good that it will come loose all at once and fly open, spilling the contents. Because you were using excessive force, you failed to feel the exact moment when the drawer loosened, and you lost control. You weren't experiencing the drawer anymore; you were instead experiencing only your own effort. This excessive effort made you more self-aware, obscured your experience of your work, and reduced your control.

It is common to see student actors make the mistake of trying too hard, and the harder they try, the worse they get. Perhaps they feel unworthy of the audience's attention unless they do something extraordinary to earn it; the option of doing nothing, of simply allowing themselves to "be there," is terrifying. They feel naked and exposed and become desperate to do something, anything! As a result, they have difficulty experiencing what is really happening on stage.

Here is the secret that will make miracles happen for you as an actor: Acting is mostly a matter of *letting go*—letting go of too much effort, letting go of chronic physical tension, letting go of a false voice, letting go of your preconceptions about the work, letting go of fear, and, most of all, letting go of who you already are in order to become someone new.

The first step in letting go is *relaxation*. For an actor, relaxation does not mean reduced energy or slackness; rather it means that all unnecessary tensions have been removed, the remaining energy has been purposefully focused, and awareness is at a high level. The kind of relaxation you want is a state in which you are most ready to react to the slightest stimulus, like a cat in front of a mouse hole. This is what meditators call *restful alertness*. You are already capable of restful alertness and you don't need to do anything to achieve it; you need only to become still enough to experience it. Do this now, through a simple meditation.

EXERCISE 2.1 A MEDITATION

Sit comfortably in your chair, both feet flat on the floor, back and neck straight but not rigid, hands resting on your thighs. Look at a spot on the floor eight feet in front of you, or if you like, close your eyes. Focus your awareness on your breath flowing in and out of your nose. Allow any thoughts that come up to play across your consciousness, and then simply return your awareness to your breath. Resist nothing. Sit for as long as you are comfortable. Whatever experience you have is correct.

The ability to relax can be learned. Psychologists speak of the "relaxation response," which develops with repetition just like any other skill. The following exercise is a classic in the field of relaxation. Although you can quickly learn it on your own, it would be useful for your teacher or a partner to lead you at first so you aren't distracted by having to read the instructions. If necessary, a tape recording of these instructions with the necessary pauses could guide you.

EXERCISE 2.2 PHASIC RELAXATION

Lie in a comfortable position, knees slightly raised and feet flat on the floor. As in your meditation, your breath is the focus of your awareness. Imagine that each inhalation is a warm, energy-filled fluid flowing into your body. Each exhalation carries away with it tension and inhibition, like a refreshing outgoing wave. Breathe deeply and easily in a slow, natural, regular rhythm.

Each successive breath will be sent into a different part of the body. As the breath flows into each area, let the muscles there tighten as much as they can; then, as the breath flows out, let the muscles release as the breath carries all the tension away with it, leaving the area refreshed and at ease. Exhaling is letting go.

The sequence of breaths moves from the top of the body to the feet. Increasingly, the regular rhythm of your breathing should make the muscular contractions and relaxations flow smoothly down the body like a slow wave. Send your breath into each of these areas in turn:

1. The *forehead and scalp*—furrowing your brow and then releasing it; keeping your eyes at rest, closed, and turned slightly downward.
2. The *jaw*—clenching it and then letting it fall easily downward until your teeth are about one-half inch apart.
3. The *tongue*—extending it and then letting it lie easily in your mouth.
4. The *front of the neck*—extending your chin down to touch your chest, stretching the back of the neck, and then rolling your head easily back.
5. The *back of the neck*—rolling the top of your head back and under to touch the floor, stretching the front of your neck, and

then rolling your head slowly back down so that the neck is longer than before.

6. The *upper chest*—swelling your chest outward in all directions so that the shoulders are widened and then letting your chest easily subside so that you feel your shoulder blades spread, wider than before.

7. The *arms and hands*—letting them become stiff and straight like steel rods, clenching your hands into fists, and then letting your hands uncurl and your arms melt into the floor.

8. The *pit of the stomach*—clenching it into a small, hard ball and then, with a sigh, releasing it.

9. The *legs and knees*—stiffening your knees as you straighten your legs, pushing your feet downward, and then releasing your legs and feeling them melt into the floor.

10. The *feet*—with the backs of your heels still touching the floor, stretching your toes up toward your chin and then releasing them, letting them fall into a natural position.

11. The *length of the body*—pushing the backs of your heels and your shoulder blades simultaneously downward into the floor so that your whole body lifts upward in a long arch and then, with a sigh, letting your body slowly fall, lengthening as it relaxes and melting deep into the floor.

12. Now take ten deep, slow, regular breaths, and with each breath move more deeply into relaxation. The flow of breath is a continuous cycle of energy that is stored comfortably in the body; with each breath, this store of energy is increased. If a yawn comes to you, enjoy it fully, and vocalize the exhalation, letting the sound of the yawn pour out.

As you repeat this exercise on successive days, you can give yourself the instructions silently. Keep a steady rhythm that follows the tempo of your deep, relaxed breathing. Gradually, the action of the exercise will become natural, and you will no longer need to think of the instructions, giving your full awareness to the flow of contractions and relaxations that follow your breath as it travels down your body like a wave—awakening, refreshing, and relaxing your body and making you ready for work. Use this exercise as an easy and quick preparation for all future work. Over a period of time, it will help break up and dissolve chronic bundles of tension within your body. Like any skill, relaxation must be developed over a period of time and maintained once achieved. Meditation and relaxation techniques are used by many actors throughout their lives.

Finding Your Center

Good acting requires that all the parts of your body, your voice, and your mind work together in an integrated way. This integration is a natural state. Even if, as you've grown up, you have learned habits of movement or voice that have made you disintegrated and awkward, you can easily rediscover your natural

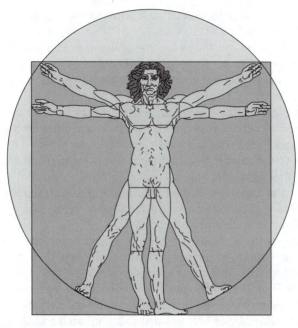

FIGURE 2.1

The Bodily Center According to Leonardo Da Vinci

wholeness. You begin by experiencing the true source of integrated movement and voice deep in the center of your body.

This idea of a personal center is not just a metaphor; it has a tangible physical dimension. There is a "pure" center deep within your body, at your center of gravity, roughly three finger-widths below your navel. (See Figure 2.1.) Cicely Berry, Voice Director of the Royal Shakespeare Company, says that the bodily center is where laughter begins, and you can feel this in yourself if you begin to laugh. It is here that the breath (and therefore the voice) originates, as well as all large motions of the body. It is the source of your greatest power. Golfers, baseball and tennis players, and many other kinds of athletes learn to initiate movement from this center, and so must the actor. The pure center is the undistorted source from which your work begins in order to develop the unique ways of using your body and voice required by whatever character you will create throughout the rest of your working process. Here is an exercise to help you develop a specific sense of your physical center.

EXERCISE 2.3 FINDING YOUR CENTER

Stand upright and relax. Clear your mind and witness your body as it performs the following activities:

1. Move either foot out to the side about two feet; then rock from foot to foot, feeling your center of gravity moving from side to

side. Quickly make your rocking motions smaller and smaller, like a bowling pin that almost falls down. Come to rest on center.

2. Move either foot forward about two feet; make front-to-back rocking motions, and again come to rest on center.
3. Move your center around rotationally, exploring the limits of various stances. Feel the weight of your body flowing out of your center, through your legs, and into the ground.
4. With one finger, point at the spot in your body that you feel is your center; don't be concerned about where it *ought* to be, but sense where it really is.
5. Explore how your center is involved in breathing, making sound, and moving.

In this exercise, you may have found that your center is not at the "pure" location just below your navel. Many of us have lost touch with this pure center and operate instead from some higher center, such as our chests. Unfortunately, when we fail to work from our lower center, we inevitably look and sound stiff and superficial, and our movements and voice will not have the fullness and expressiveness needed for performance. You may need to repeat this exercise over a period of days and weeks, letting your sense of center drop until the pure center starts to feel natural to you.

As you become aware of your center over a period of days, you will notice that it moves within your body as your mood changes; frequently, your center will rise upward when you are in an excited or fearful state, or downward in states of well-being or determination. You will notice, too, that different people have different characteristic centers and that the locations of their centers are very appropriate to their personalities. Such diversity can be found in people who have a "lot of guts" or who "follow their noses," "lead with their chins," are "all heart," "drag their feet," "have their heads in the clouds," and so on. Although we begin our work from our ideal center, there is no "correct" voice or posture for a performance until these are determined by the demands of the role. Later, in Step 10, you will use the placement of center as a way of exploring the physical aspects of characterization.

Breathing, Sounding, and Moving From Center

The relaxation exercise (Exercise 2.2) focused on breath for a very good reason: Breath is life. The word "psychology" means "study of the soul," and the word for soul, "psyche," originally meant "vital breath." Think about it: When you breathe, you are bringing the outside world into your body and then sending it out again. Your breath therefore constantly reflects your relationship to your world. When you are frightened, you hold your breath because you don't want to let the threatening world in. When you are happy, your breath flows freely. The way you feel about your world is expressed in the way you breathe it in and breathe it out.

For this reason your natural voice, which is based on your breath, expresses your inner state. Speaking—as well as sobbing, laughing, gasping, sighing, and all the other sounds you make—is the natural and automatic reflection of your relationship to your world. Consequently, actors are careful not to force their voices into unnatural and artificial patterns and often work hard to free their natural voices from bad habits. Unfortunately, the influence of television has turned many of us into "talking heads," causing us to lose touch with the natural breathing and vocal processes that begin deep inside our bodies. Here is an exercise that will help you to experience the natural integration of breath, body, and voice that occurs when we learn to operate from the pure lower center.

EXERCISE 2.4   **BREATHING AND SOUNDING FROM YOUR CENTER**

1. Sit comfortably in your chair, or lie on the floor. Relax yourself by allowing your breath to sweep through your body as in the relaxation exercise (Exercise 2.2). As you breathe easily and slowly, become aware that your breath is rising and falling from a deep place in your body, a little below your navel.
2. As your breath travels outward from this deep place, make sound lightly; do not disturb your breath, and just allow it to vibrate, as it may sometimes do just as you are falling asleep. This is your natural voice—your vibrating breath carrying energy from deep within you into the outside world. Open your throat by yawning; the yawn can be a great help in removing tension.
3. Reach effortlessly with your vibrating breath into the world around you. Put yourself, randomly, into new positions and experience the vibrating breath flowing through each. What changes occur in your voice?
4. As you continue to produce sound, feel the vibrations of that sound spreading into every part of your body: out of the neck and into the head and chest; into the back, the stomach, the buttocks; into the arms and hands; into the legs and feet; and into the scalp. Feel the sound radiating from every part of your body. With the touch of a light fingertip, check every surface of your body. Are there "dead spots" that are not participating in the sound?

Examine your experience during this exercise: Did you have a new sense of the capacity of your entire body to join in the act of sounding? Did you feel more in touch with yourself and with the space around you, as if your sound were literally reaching outside yourself in a tangible way? Are you now more alert, refreshed, and relaxed? You have begun to experience how the body, voice, and mind are all integral to one another, and breath is the great unifier that binds them all together.

The Cycle of Energy

Whenever you try to do something, to achieve some objective—that is, whenever you *act*—you send energy flowing out from your center into the outer world in the form of sound, speech, gesture, or movement. In a scene, your action provokes a reaction from the other character and you in turn again receive this new energy from them. This incoming energy flows into you and touches your center, which in turn elicits a further reaction from you, and so on. It is this flow of energy from character to character through the cycle of action and reaction that makes a scene unfold.

This idea of a cycle of energy is central to Asian martial arts such as *tai chi chuan*, and study in these arts can be of great benefit to an actor. Here is an exercise taken from yoga that will let you experience the cycle of energy.

EXERCISE 2.5 YOUR CYCLE OF ENERGY

Sit on the floor with your back straight, and spread your legs a little with the knees slightly raised. (See Figure 2.2.) Feel as if you are being lifted from your center and out through the top of your head so that your back and neck are long and wide. Keep your head level, your eyes looking straight ahead, and your waist level as well.

1. As you breathe out, reach forward and down with your arms and torso, keeping your back and neck long and your shoulders wide. Imagine yourself in a large theater, bowing to someone sitting in the last row.
2. As you breathe in, use your arms and hands to gather your breath into the lower part of your body, scooping "energy" into the funnel formed by your legs.
3. As your breath begins to fill you, feel its warmth and power flowing up within you. Follow its upward movement with your hands, so that your arms scoop the energy in and upward as if you are embracing it.
4. As your breath rises in your body, let it lift you, straightening and lengthening your upper torso and neck, lifting your head, and widening your shoulders and throat as it flows upward like a wave moving through you in a slow undulation. Let yourself unfurl like a fern opening.
5. That breath then flows into the outer world; give an "ah" sound to that imaginary person sitting at the back of the theater, and accompany it with an unfolding gesture of the arms toward the person.
6. As the power of that breath begins to diminish, close your mouth so the "ah" sound becomes an "oh" and then an "m," and experience a tingling sensation in your mouth and nose areas. The smooth flow of the sound produces a trisyllable word, "ah-oh-m," or *om*.
7. As your breath and sound die away, let your body again bow forward and down and your arms reach forward to scoop in a new quantity of breath energy, as the cycle begins again.
8. Repeat the cycle several times, feeling the continuity of inward and outward breaths so the entire exercise becomes one unbroken, flowing experience with no sharp corners.

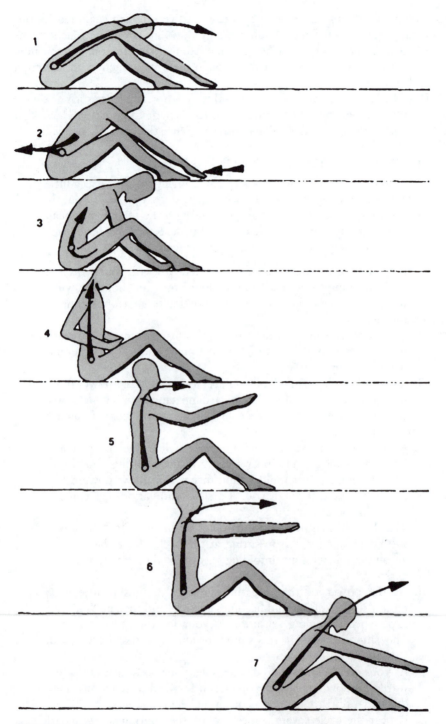

FIGURE 2.2
The Cycle of Energy

Your Relationship to Gravity

You live in specific relationship to gravity, and you move and sound within that relationship. Like your breathing, the way you experience gravity is a fundamental expression of your relationship to your world. Some days it seems that you wake up heavier, with "the weight of the world" on your shoulders, and you feel "down"; at the saddest times you say you have a "heavy heart." On the other hand, sometimes you feel "up" or "light-hearted." When you are sure of yourself, you feel as if you are receiving strength from gravity, and you speak of "knowing where I stand" or "holding my ground."

People's attitudes toward gravity can be seen in their postures. When Arthur Miller opens his play *Death of a Salesman* with Willy Loman crossing the stage, back bent under the weight of his sample case, Willy's sense of defeat and hopelessness is directly expressed in the way he is losing his fight with gravity. In musical theater, in contrast, it is a convention that lovers actually defy gravity by skipping, as if they were about to float away "on cloud nine." Here is an exercise to help you discover the various ways in which you experience gravity.

> EXERCISE 2.6 ROOTS
>
> Imagine yourself standing on a mirror; below you is your other self with its own center. Imagine a bond between your center "up here" and the one "down there" in your mirror image. This imaginary bond of energy is like a root. As you move, your root moves with you; you can even "detach" your root. Try the following movements, but don't act them out; simply experience them through these images, and discover what they feel like.
>
> 1. Select a destination; detach and lift your root, move to the destination, and replant your root there.
> 2. Now move to a destination without lifting your root, plowing a furrow through the ground as you move. Feel yourself pushing your whole body through space. We will call this *molding*.
> 3. Now lift your root, and leave it dangling the whole time, whether moving or standing still. We will call this *floating*.
> 4. Now imagine the root being drawn upward, still attached at your center, but lifting your center upward and out through the top of your head. Move with the sense that you have to reach down to touch the floor; you are *flying*.

There are distinct differences among the experiences of molding, floating, and flying, and each of them might express several different things: Molding, for instance, can express dejection or defeat, but it might also express determination or commitment; floating can express joy or enthusiasm, but it might also express confusion or vulnerability.

Although these bodily conditions, which are called the bodily *dynamic*, change as mood and emotion changes, people also have a characteristic way of experiencing gravity that is usual to them and from which they depart as their moods change, and this characteristic dynamic is profoundly expressive of character. In Step 10, you will experiment with adjustments in bodily dynamic, as well as the placement of center, as techniques useful to the creation of the bodily aspects of characterization.

Begin to observe in everyday life how the position of people's bodily centers and their relationships to gravity express their personalities. I encourage you to record your observations in an acting journal, noting expressive postures, gestures, and utterances you observe in daily life. Many actors find a journal useful not only to record such observations but also to record experiences and ideas that result from their work as actors.

Summary of Step 2

For most of us, performing arouses anxiety. This makes us tense, interferes with our ability to react, and reduces our creativity. For all these reasons, tension is the greatest enemy of the creative state, and the first step toward that creative state is to relax. When we speak of relaxation for an actor, we do not mean the ordinary sense of reduced energy or slackness, but rather a state in which all unnecessary tensions have been removed, energy has been purposefully focused, and awareness is at a high level. This is what meditators call "restful alertness."

Besides being relaxed, actors also need to be whole, because good acting requires that all the parts of the body, voice, and mind work together in an integrated way. The true source of integrated movement and voice is deep within the center of the body, roughly three finger-widths below the navel. It is here that breath (and therefore voice), as well as laughter, all large motions of the body, and all the deepest impulses originate. The pure center is an undistorted source from which to begin our work and develop in any way required by a role. Eventually, we will find the center appropriate to the character.

When you breathe, you are bringing the outside world into your body and then sending it out again. Your breath constantly reflects your relationship to your world. Your natural voice, originating in your breath, automatically expresses your inner world.

You experience your center in specific relationship to gravity, and you move and sound within that relationship. Consequently, the way you experience gravity is also a fundamental expression of your relationship to your world. Three of the ways we experience gravity are called molding, floating, and flying. Our experience of gravity expresses our attitude toward the world and changes as our feelings change. Although these bodily conditions, which are called the bodily *dynamic*, change as mood and emotion changes, people also have a characteristic way of experiencing gravity that is usual to them and from which they depart as their moods change, and this characteristic dynamic is profoundly expressive of character.

STEP 3

Your Voice and Speech

LEARNING OBJECTIVES

- Explore the workings of your vocal mechanism, beginning with basic breath support and the production of sound.
- Follow the sound you produce as it is articulated into the sounds produced by the actions of your jaw, tongue, nasal passages, and the other mechanism that produced good articulated speech.
- Explore the conditions that affect both your voice and speech and express your character and his or her situation.

Some scholars have called human speech an "overlaid function," meaning that it is an activity that the human race has developed using muscles and organs that first evolved for other, more basic purposes: The diaphragm and lungs developed for breathing, the larynx for swallowing, the tongue, the teeth, and the lips for chewing, and the palate and tongue for tasting. Thus, speech is connected to our most basic survival activities. It is our most expressive and our most uniquely human activity.

As you experienced in Step 2, your voice begins as breath coming from deep in the center of your body; by the time your voice reaches the outside world, it has travelled through many essential structures and automatically carries with it an expression of the condition of your inner state of being. In fact, the voice expresses our inner life so well that it is difficult to disguise deep feelings when we speak; on the other hand, a lack of real inner feeling will result in an unconvincing delivery no matter how hard we try to fake emotion by vocal tricks. Ultimately, when you speak or make noises, you are actually "turning yourself inside out." It is no accident that the root of the word "personality" is *per sona*, "through sound."

EXERCISE 3.1   **RUNNING ON THE INSIDE**

Stand and run in place, lifting your knees high and letting your arms pump vigorously. Count every other step in a loud voice; when you reach 30, stop running "outside" and stand very still, but continue to run "inside" while you go on counting to 50. Can you hear how your voice reflects the inner condition of your body even when there is no external motion?

Just as your voice reflected your inner activity in this exercise, it reflects also the vocal symptoms of emotion, such as sobbing or laughing, even if these are not yet visible. Some even call speech an "overflow" activity, something we do when our internal dynamic is high; for example, singers in opera or musical theater know that it takes a high level of inner energy to justify breaking into song. Speech on the stage must also be supported by a rich inner arousal.

It is important to realize that the connection between your inner world and your voice works in both directions; speech comes out of you, but it can also in a sense go into you. A playwright, unlike any other kind of writer, knows that his or her words will be spoken aloud by an actor. The good playwright therefore gives us words to speak that make the thoughts and feelings they express believable; not only because of their meaning but also because of the sounds, rhythms, and sensations they carry. If you can make a strong connection between your inner life and the act of speaking, the power of the writer's words can reach into you and help to create the inner world of the character as the writer envisioned it. In this way, the old British acting tradition that advised, "Just say the words," may not have been entirely off the mark, as long as we realize that "saying the words" can be a profound and total action of our entire being with powerful psychological and spiritual results.

Using Your Own Voice

Building a strong connection between your inner life and your voice assumes that your voice is allowed to function in its natural, undistorted way. But sometimes actors choose to adopt an artificial voice for the sake of "creating a character," or "playing age," or, especially with Shakespeare, "being poetic." If you do this, your voice will no longer be authentically personal and the connection between your inner life and your speech will be destroyed. Your aim is to enter into the life of the character, and you make that journey first and most actively by saying what the character says. If you do not say it with your own voice you will be cut off from this primary point of entry into the experience of the character. While it is true that your voice may undergo some degree of transformation in the course of working on a role, this transformation must be the result of other, deeper changes that cannot be replaced by vocal fakery.

It may be difficult for you to be comfortable performing in your own voice. Because the voice is so revealing of our inner life, there is a strong ego identification with it. When we feel exposed while performing, there is an impulse to avoid "being there" by hiding behind a false voice. As Cicely Berry, voice director of the Royal Shakespeare Company says, "we have to practice ways of feeling at home with the voice, of hearing your own vibration, of what I call 'sitting down' in it."[1] Following is an exercise adapted from her book, *Text in Action*.

For this exercise select one of the speeches from Shakespeare in Appendix C that moves you personally in some way. This speech should be thoroughly memorized and will be used for this and several of the following exercises.

EXERCISE 3.2   SITTING DOWN IN YOUR VOICE

Work with a partner. One of you sits on a chair and the other sits on the floor immediately in front of them facing away.

1. Those on the chair, support partner's back with your hands. Those on the floor, feel your weight on the floor, and then lean gently back against your partner for support. Those on chair, feel partner's weight.
2. Those on floor, put one hand on your stomach and "breathe down," from the lower abdomen. Feel your breath settle, and then breathe out making an "F" sound so that you feel the flow of a channel of air from your deep center into the outside world. Then change the sound to a "V" and feel the vibration spread throughout your body. As you do this, your partner helps you to feel your weight and your centered voice, and you both feel the resonance of the vibrating sound.
3. Begin to speak your selection, keeping this same deep centeredness. Give yourself over to the meaning and music of the speech.
4. Now stand and deliver your speech to the group, keeping the comfortable feeling of "sitting" in your voice.
5. Switch places and repeat the exercise.
6. Could you hear the difference in your voice when you got comfortable "sitting" in it? Were you able to carry that experience into your delivery to the group? Did the words of the speech affect you? Did you find yourself naturally engaged in their meaning and feeling?

Speech

Humankind was once described as "the animal who talks." Speech is an amazing capacity: It begins with our most fundamental experience of pleasure and pain. We see this in the development of each infant as he or she learns to talk. In the earliest stage of development, the baby makes noises that express its feelings: gurgles of pleasure or cries of hunger. The baby also explores the world by

---

[1]Cicely Berry, *Text in Action* (London: Virgin Publishing Ltd., 2001), p. 94.

grabbing it and literally "taking it in" to its mouth. Later, the baby notices that making certain sounds makes mommy appear, or causes food to be given. The baby soon realizes that *the voice can reach farther than the hand*; it realizes that it can affect the world by producing certain sounds, and with this realization the capacity for speech is born.

Viewed in this way, speech is a special kind of doing; it is the most specific way in which we send our energies into the world in our effort to satisfy our needs. This is a particularly useful view of speech for the actor. In creating a play, the writer has channeled a total human situation full of feelings and actions into the relatively few words of the dialogue. When you speak that dialogue on stage, you must re-create the full condition, including the actions, from which the words come; your voice must be *doing*; your words should be hitting, or caressing, or grabbing, or whatever the action underlying the speech may be. The actor, then, thinks of speech as a muscular process whereby feelings, needs, and thoughts find their expression in articulated sound, sound that is intended to produce a real effect on the world.

As you form your thoughts into the physical activity called speech, you make a great many choices that are expressive of your feelings, needs, values, background, and personality. In this way, your *process of verbalization* expresses the kind of person you are and the way in which you try to cope with your world. It is this living quality of speech *coming to be for the first time* that you must relive as you work on your character's words. If you deliver your lines merely as memorized words, you deprive yourself of the transformational power of participating actively in the character's thought processes that lie behind the words he or she speaks. The words of the dialogue are both your starting point and your final destination: You "take them apart" in rehearsal to discover the thoughts and feelings that drive them; in performance you relive these thoughts and feelings and the words come out "under their own power."

EXERCISE 3.3 **BRINGING A SPEECH TO LIFE**

Using your memorized monologue, go through it to experience the thoughts and feelings that drive the words; allow the words of the speech to form gradually, like a picture coming into focus. Do this with each phrase or sentence, letting the words come from the need to communicate the idea or feeling involved. Does a sense of character begin to emerge as you experience the character's words coming to life?

Voice Production

In the rest of this step, we will follow the voice from its source through the journey it takes within the body until it finally reaches the outside world as articulated speech. You already know that the voice is "vibrating breath" that begins in your deepest center. The system that produces the breath consists of the diaphragm and lungs, which act as a kind of "bellows." This bellows system

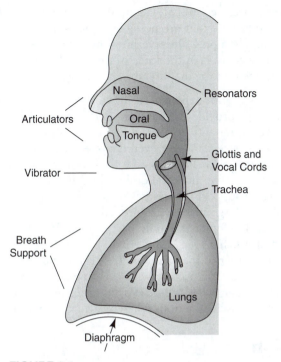

FIGURE 3.1
The Vocal Apparatus

operates simply: As the diaphragm (see Figure 3.1) pulls downward in the chest cavity, air is drawn into the lungs. As it relaxes and moves upward, the air is driven through the bronchial tubes and trachea, through the pharynx and then into the throat, mouth, and nasal chambers.

EXERCISE 3.4   BREATH AND VOICE

1. Relax in a standing position and quickly send your breath throughout your body, as in your relaxation exercise. Give yourself a good shaking and let all tensions go.

2. Place your hands about 6 inches above your waist and breathe slowly, deeply, and fully. Feel the motion of your diaphragm as your whole torso expands and contracts. Is it unduly tense, causing its movement to be limited and erratic? Concentrate on eliminating tension here. Check also the areas at the sides of the lower back; are you breathing and responding all the way around your abdomen? Are you using the entire central section of your body to breathe, or are you a "chest breather" who depends only on the limited capacity of the upper torso?

3. Now, roll your head and shoulders to free them, and then let a full yawn pour out of you, opening your throat.

4. Now produce a continual vocalized tone and explore the variations in that tone that are possible through manipulation of the breath supply alone. Observe how the resonance of the tone is affected by changes in the force of the breath and by controlling the movement of the diaphragm.

In this exercise, you experienced how the "bellows" formed by the diaphragm and lungs provide the basic support for your breath and therefore for your voice. You rarely utilize, in real life, even half of your potential reservoir of air, nor do the demands of everyday speech cause you to develop the muscles that activate this bellows system to anywhere near its full potential. The serious stage actor will undertake special study and long-term exercise to develop good breath support that relates directly to the ability to "project" the voice effortlessly in a large space when needed.

This muscular development is only part of what is needed, however; more important is good *articulation*. Many young actors think that being heard in larger theaters is a matter of speaking *loudly*; it is much more a matter of speaking *purposefully and clearly*. Actors with even modest voices can be heard in large theaters when they have well-developed articulation. We turn now to the series of places and muscular actions whereby articulation is achieved.

Articulation

First comes the point at which the breath is vibrated and becomes sound. In this, your body works just like any other wind instrument. The outpouring column of air causes vibration as it passes through the vocal cords. This vibration sets the column of air in motion and the vibration is thus resonated and amplified. It is then changed in quality (articulated) as it passes through the mouth and nose.

This natural process, unless you resist or distort it in some way, will automatically insure the organic unity of breath, voice, emotion, and activity. However, tension in the throat area will adversely influence the operation of the vocal cords, unnecessarily restrict the flow of breath, producing a strident and unnatural sound, and will soon cause a sore throat. It will also detract from a performance since no muscular tension is communicated to an audience as quickly as a tense or sore throat.

When we consider how the vocal cords operate, we see that they are capable of four basic movements:

1. When the vocal cords are drawn fully apart so that the air stream is permitted to pass through them unhindered, we produce the quality of speech called "voicelessness."
2. When they are closed and tensed, the air stream is forced through them, and they vibrate like reeds in the wind, producing tone. By increasing or decreasing their tension, we increase or decrease pitch.
3. By a quick closing, the vocal cords can interrupt the breath stream suddenly and entirely, resulting in a "glottal stop."
4. There is also a stage somewhere between the first and second that produces a semi-voiced tone called "stage whisper."

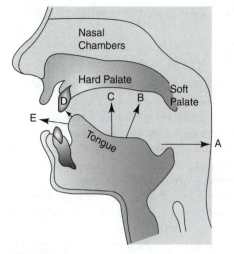

FIGURE 3.2

Points of Articulation: (A) Guttural, (B) Rear Palatal, (C) Middle Palatal, (D) Dental, (E) Labial

EXERCISE 3.5   **VOICED AND VOICELESS SOUNDS**

The vocal cords either "voice" the breath stream or allow it to pass freely as a "voiceless" sound. For example, **B** and **P** are articulated in exactly the same manner, except **B** is voiced and **P** is not; likewise, **D** is voiced while **T** is not. Try producing each of these types of sound as you say very slowly, "the **b**oy has a **p**ony and the **d**og has a **t**oy." Lightly touch your throat and feel it change.

Next, as the breath stream, whether voiced or not, passes beyond the pharynx, it encounters three further forms of articulation. (See Figure 3.2.) First, the soft palate may raise or lower to direct the breath either into the nose or into the mouth; then, if the breath flows into the mouth, it is either impeded, or allowed to pass freely; finally, if it is impeded, the location of the point at which it is impeded produces a particular sound. Here are the possibilities:

1. Does the breath pass into the nasal or oral chamber?
2. If the oral chamber, is the breath impeded?
3. If impeded, at what point is it interrupted?

   Let's briefly explore each of these in turn.

Nasal Sounds

The first point beyond the vocal cords at which the breath stream is articulated is at the soft palate near the rear of the mouth. As this soft palate lowers or raises, it opens or closes the pathway by which the air stream may pass into the nasal cavity where it is given a special resonance. In English we

have only three basic sounds that depend upon nasal resonance: *m, n,* and
ng (as in si*ng*).

EXERCISE 3.6   **NASAL SOUNDS**

1. While producing a continual open tone (e.g., *a* as in f*a*ther), open
   and close the soft palate (turning the sound of *a* into *ng*), and feel
   the vibrations produced in your throat, mouth, and the triangular
   area of your face surrounding your nose. Try to project the nasal
   tone into this triangular area (sometimes called *the mask*) so that
   the surface vibrations in this area can be felt with the fingertips.
2. With the open vowel sound of *a* being formed in the mouth, see
   how much resonance the nasal cavity contributes even to nonnasal
   sounds. Check this by snapping the nostrils open and shut between
   your fingers as you make the vowel sound. Project the tone toward
   the front of the face, producing strong vibrations in the mask.

Oral Sounds: Vowels and Diphthongs

The most complex acts of articulation take place inside the mouth. The breath
stream, voiced or unvoiced, may be allowed to pass freely or it may be impeded
in some way; if it passes freely, it may be "shaped" by the positioning of the
mouth's movable parts (mainly the jaw, tongue, and lips). The sounds produced
in this "open" fashion are the *vowels*.

The vowel sounds used in English fall into four categories: those produced by
shaping the mouth at the front (with the lips), the middle (with the tongue), or the
back (using rear of the tongue and the jaw). There are also combination sounds
called "diphthongs" that are unbroken glides from one vowel sound to another.

EXERCISE 3.7   **VOWELS AND DIPHTHONGS**

1. Relax and open your throat. Say each of these sentences slowly,
   exaggerating the "shape" of the mouth in producing each sound.
   Read the sentences in order, concentrating on the movement from
   front to rear in the mouth, and on the increasing "size" as more
   and more space is created within the mouth.

   FRONT: W*e* w*i*ll m*a*ke th*e*m m*a*d f*a*st.
   MIDDLE: *U*p f*u*rther, f*u*rther.
   BACK: Ch*a*rles w*a*nts *a*ll *o*ld b*oo*ks t*oo*.

2. Now speak the diphthongs in this sentence in slow motion,
   exploring the gliding motion from one vowel sound to another.
   At first, exaggerate a clearly distinguishable sound for each
   vowel, as in "Maa-ee" for "May."

   M*ay I* j*oi*n y*ou* n*ow*, J*oe*?

3. Deliver your memorized practice speech so as to emphasize
   the vowel sounds, especially any that are emphasized by bring

repeated (*assonance*) or that have special sound values that convey mood or meaning.

Consonants

When the breath stream is impeded or interrupted in the mouth, the resulting sounds are the *consonants*. The consonants are necessarily less resonant and more incisive than the vowels. The word "consonant" originally meant "sounding with," because these sounds alone cannot comprise a syllable; they must be combined with a vowel.

There are four principal positions within the mouth at which the articulation of consonants may occur (see Figure 3.2):

A. *Guttural:* The rear of the tongue reaches toward the back of the mouth. Guttural sounds appear in some languages (like the *ch* in the Yiddish "*Ch*annukah"), but in English guttural sounds are used only in nonverbal noises.
B. *Rear Palatal:* The rear of the tongue may rise up to make contact with the soft palate to make sounds like "*g*un."
C. *Middle Palatal:* A slightly more forward sound may be produced by the middle of the tongue rising up to contact the roof of the mouth as in "*k*ey."
D. *Dental:* Here the tongue touches either the bony ridge directly behind the upper teeth (as in the sound "*t*ea") or the teeth themselves (as in the sound "*th*ese").
E. *Labial:* The lips may be in contact with each other (as in "*b*oy") or the lower lip touches the upper teeth (as in "*f*riend").

Notice that in each position different sounds are produced by either voicing or not voicing the tone without any other alteration.

At any of these points the breath stream may be entirely interrupted, or only partly impeded. When the breath stream is entirely interrupted, the result is called a *plosive* since the breath stream is cut off and then "explodes" suddenly (*b*oy). When the breath is only partly impeded, the result is a *continuant* because these sounds can be extended (*l*ovely). There are several kinds of continuants: *nasals* (si*ng*), *fricatives* (when the breath flows through a narrow passageway as in *f*riend), those with a hissing quality called *sibilants* (*s*orry), *blends* (*ch*oice, *J*oy), *glides* including *laterals* (*l*ovely), and *liquids* (*r*at).

EXERCISE 3.8   **CONSONANTS**

Using your monologue, speak it slowly to explore the movement and shape of the mouth required to produce each consonant. Exaggerate the movement needed to produce each sound. Pay special attention to any sounds that are emphasized by being repeated (*alliteration*). Are you producing a distinctly different sound for each? Are regional peculiarities or bad speech habits affecting any of your sounds? Is the muscular action of your jaw, tongue, and lips precise enough to produce clean sounds? Can you feel how much you will need to practice this skill until it becomes effortless and natural?

Speech, Character, and Situation

Situation and especially our relationship to others have an enormous impact on articulation. Imagine the same words spoken in a public forum, or secretly to an intimate friend, or in a dangerous situation, or to someone we hate, or someone we love. This is why context must always be considered when judging the expressiveness of speech. For example, an evenness of accent and pitch may indicate timidity or quiet authority; a voice extremely active in both range and dynamics may express hysteria or joy; the emphasizing of hard, biting sounds may indicate anger or excitement; the elongation of open vowel sounds may indicate pleasure or pain.

Your study of the voice is aimed at creating a flexible and responsive instrument that will help you to express character within the character's situation. Along with the development of your technical control of articulation, you also want to develop your "ear," that is, your ability to hear the expressive aspects of speech in real life.

EXERCISE 3.9 **SPEECH IN LIFE**

Observe around you the speech of all sorts of people.

1. How are laziness, timidity, aggressiveness, pompousness, stupidity, and many other personality traits expressed by speech and especially articulation?
2. What effect do various emotions have on speech?
3. What effect does situation have on speech?
4. Use your monologue to re-create the patterns you have observed to deliver it as it might be spoken by various kinds of people in various situations and emotional states.
   A. An angry bully.
   B. A frightened lover.
   C. A passionate believer.
   D. Someone passing on an important secret.
   E. Other of your own invention.

   What feelings does the monologue inspire in you when you speak in these various ways?

Further Training of Body and Voice

Steps 2 and 3 have briefly explored the most basic expressive skills of the actor. Advanced training in movement, voice, and speech goes far beyond what has been suggested here, and anyone serious about an acting career must seek further specialized study. It is important to do this work with a qualified teacher, for bad habits are easy to learn and difficult to undo. There are several approaches to vocal and bodily training that yield good results, but no matter what approach is taken, the aim is always to liberate, expand, and utilize the capacities of your natural body and voice. For serious actors, this is a lifelong study.

Opportunities to explore related training in such skills as mime, singing, dancing, clowning, fencing, Tai Chi Chu'an and other Oriental martial arts, tumbling, and meditation may also be valuable. Each contributes in its way to useful acting skills and, more importantly, to the spiritual dimension of acting—for these physical disciplines develop also the mind, emotions, and imagination, and thereby liberate the actor's creative spirit.

Summary of Step 3

Speech begins when a baby notices that the voice can reach farther than the hand. Viewed in this way, speech is a special kind of doing; it is the most specific way in which we send our energies into the world in our effort to satisfy our needs. On stage, especially, speech is a form of doing.

Think of speech as a physical process whereby feelings, needs, and thoughts find their expression in muscular activity that produces articulated sound. The word personality comes from the root per sona, meaning "through sound." The act of speaking literally turns you inside out. Playwrights write not for the eye but for the human voice; the words your character speaks reflects his or her thoughts and feelings and your ability to re-create his or her speech is a fundamental first step in your creation of the character. It is therefore important that you avoid any artificial distortion of your voice when you act, because you make the journey into the character's mind first and most actively by saying what the character says; if you do not say it with your own voice you will be cut off from this fundamental point of entry into the character.

The "bellows" formed by the diaphragm and lungs create the breath stream that is the source of the voice. The breath then passes through the vocal cords which can produce either a "voiced" or a "voiceless" sound. The breath stream, voiced or unvoiced, passes beyond the pharynx where the soft palate may raise or lower to direct the breath either into the nose or the mouth; then, if the breath flows into the mouth, it is either impeded, or allowed to pass freely; finally, if it is impeded, the location of the point at which it is impeded produces a particular sound.

Like every aspect of the voice, articulation is profoundly expressive of personality, feeling, and situation, especially of relationship, and must always be understood in context.

A career in acting requires the development of skills of body, voice, and speech that are, for most actors, a lifelong study and practice.

STEP 4

Working Together

LEARNING OBJECTIVES

- Experience directly through physical exercises the sharing and exchange of energy between actors necessary to effective collaboration.
- Discover how working together requires physical, vocal, and psychological openness to your fellow actors, and a spirit of shared purpose and alignment toward the creation of a unified performance.

Actors always collaborate, literally "labor together," with others. They work not only with other actors but also with directors, stage managers, costume and makeup people, and many others. The success of any collaborative artistic endeavor depends on the ability of these many kinds of artists to work together toward the common goal of bringing the material to life.

When a group works together in the best possible way, the energy of each member of the group flows into a common stream, forming a single energy that is greater than the sum of its parts. This is why everyone on the team receives more energy from the group than he or she gives to it; we can do our best work when we are part of a well-functioning team. Furthermore, no member of the team needs to sacrifice their individuality; rather, each member finds his or her individual power enhanced by membership in the group.

Such ideal teamwork is achieved when five conditions have been met:

1. Each member is genuinely *committed* to being a member of the team.
2. Each member *supports* the work of the others.
3. There is *trust* and *mutual respect* within the team.
4. All members agree to maintain free and open *communication*.
5. The efforts of all members are *aligned* with the common purpose.

Let's examine each of these.

Commitment

It is part of your responsibility as an actor to be committed on five levels at once:

1. To *your own talent*—to being as good as you can be
2. To each *role* you play—to finding the truth of the character and of each moment in the performance
3. To each *ensemble* of which you are a member—to contributing to the success and growth of everyone in it
4. To each piece of *material* you perform—to finding and expressing the truth it contains
5. To your *audience* and the *world* you serve through your work

Support for Your Partners

We all have different reasons for working in the theater, but we support each other's objectives, even if we do not share them. We assume a nonjudgmental attitude.

Trust and Mutual Respect

We respect other workers as a matter of principle; we treat them exactly as we would want to be treated ourselves. We trust all of our partners to do their jobs, even if we disagree with their methods; we do our best to accept and utilize their contributions. If this eventually proves to be impossible, we seek resolution through respectful but honest and direct negotiation.

Free and Open Communication

No matter how supportive, trustful, and respectful we all are, creative collaboration is difficult, and we are bound to encounter differences of opinion, conflicting needs, and artistic challenges. All these problems can become opportunities for creativity as long as we can communicate freely and reasonably about them.

Alignment

When every member of the team shares a common purpose, each is free to work in his or her own way and still contribute to the overall effort. People with very different artistic methods—as well as different political, religious, cultural, and artistic values—can work in alignment toward a common purpose as long as the common purpose is well understood by all and the other four conditions listed here have been met.

Commitment, support, trust and respect, communication, and *alignment*—these are the cornerstones of teamwork, and they all require that you keep your attention on the job at hand and *park your ego at the rehearsal room door.*

Here are four enjoyable exercises that explore these qualities on a literal, physical level.

FIGURE 4.1
Falling Exercise

EXERCISE 4.1   **FALLING**

1. After everyone picks a partner, stand three feet behind your partner, keeping one foot back for stability (see Figure 4.1). By mutual agreement, your partner will start to fall backward, keeping his or her body straight but not stiff. Catch your partner right away, and gently raise him or her back up.
2. Repeat the exercise, allowing your partner to fall gradually farther and farther, until he or she falls to about four feet above the floor. If your partner becomes frightened, reassure him or her.
3. Reverse roles and repeat.

Caution: Do not attempt this exercise unless you are confident of being able to catch your partner; otherwise, serious injury could result.

EXERCISE 4.2   **FLOATING**

1. Form groups of seven or nine with one person becoming the "floater." The floaters lie flat on the floor, close their eyes, and fold their arms across their chests. The others kneel beside them, three or four on either side, and prepare to lift them (see Figure 4.2A).
2. Everyone begins to breathe in unison. When the breathing rhythm is established, the group *gently and slowly* lifts the floater, keeping him or her perfectly level. Those being lifted should feel as if they are floating.

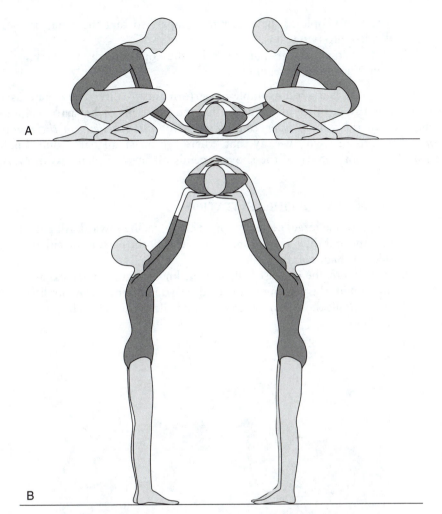

FIGURE 4.2
Floating Exercise

3. Lift the floater as high as possible while still keeping him or her level (see Figure 4.2B).
4. Slowly lower the floater, rocking him or her gently back and forth, like a leaf settling to earth.
5. Repeat with each member of the group.

Now let's use our collaborative skills to create a group scene.

EXERCISE 4.3   TUG OF WAR

1. Each member of the group creates—in pantomime—a piece of rope about two feet long.
2. Standing in a single long line, each member "attaches" his or her rope to the pieces on either side, creating one long rope.

3. The two people at the center move apart so that the group is divided into two teams.
4. Have a tug of war, but don't let the rope stretch or break. Continue until one team wins.

This exercise is a good example of performance reality: The rope ceases to be real if any member of the group fails to make his or her part real and connected to the whole. *Every individual actor must believe in the whole rope.* This explains why we say that "there are no small parts, only small actors." The total reality of the show depends on the completeness of every element in it.

EXERCISE 4.4 **GROUP LEVITATION**

1. Stand in one large, perfectly round circle, facing inward. All participants put their arms around the waists of the persons on either side (see Figure 4.3).
2. Start to breathe in unison. Bend your knees slightly when exhaling, and lift the person on either side as you breathe in. Do not lift yourself; lift those you are holding, and allow yourself to be lifted by them.

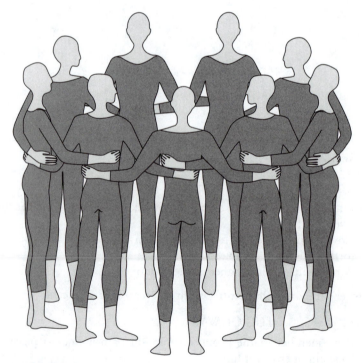

FIGURE 4.3
Group Levitation

3. As you breathe out, say the word *higher*, and try to lift those you are holding higher and higher. Allow the rhythm of the group to accelerate naturally until you all *leave the ground*.

Do you see how this exercise symbolizes the way we work together? When the energy of every member of the group is connected to the common goal and there is a basis of mutual trust, respect, and open communication, the result is greater than the sum of its parts: Everyone gets more energy back than he or she gives!

Leading and Following

When an ensemble is functioning well, energy flows easily among all the members. The roles of leader and follower are constantly changing so smoothly that it is difficult to say at any moment who is a leader and who is a follower; rather, it seems that everyone is leading and following at once. The following exercises will give you the experience of this simultaneous leading and following.

EXERCISE 4.5   LEADING AND FOLLOWING

1. *Blind leading.* You and your partner lightly interlace your fingertips up to the first joint. Your partner closes his or her eyes, and you silently lead him or her around the room. As you gain confidence and control, you can begin to move faster and extend the range of your travels. Soon you can run! If your situation permits, you can even take a trip to some distant destination. Then you can reverse roles and repeat for the trip back.
2. *Sound leading.* Begin as in No. 1, but when you are well under way, break physical contact and begin to lead your partner by repeating a single word, which your partner follows by sound alone. Again, extend your range and speed. Run! *Caution: Be prepared to grab your partner to prevent a collision.*

Review the experience of this exercise. As a follower, did you trust your partner enough to truly commit your weight to your movement? As a leader, did you receive your partner's energy and respond to his or her momentum?

Let's continue with another exercise to explore simultaneous leading and following.

EXERCISE 4.6   MIRRORS

1. You and a partner decide who is A and who is B. Stand facing each other. Person A makes slow "underwater" movements that B can mirror completely. Try to keep the partnership moving in unison. The movements should flow in a continually changing stream, avoiding repeated patterns. Bigger, more continuous movements are easier to follow.

2. At a signal, the roles are instantly reversed *without a break in the action*. B is now the leader; A is the follower. Continue moving from the deep centers of your bodies; feel yourselves beginning to share a common center through your shared movement, from which come a common breathing and a common sound that arise naturally from your movement.

3. The roles are reversed a few more times; each time the leadership role changes, the movement and sound continue without interruption.

4. Finally, there is no leader. Neither A nor B leads, but you and your partner continue to move and sound together.

Watch other partnerships doing this exercise: Do you see how intense and connected to each other they seem? Our listening to and seeing each other in performance should always have this kind of intensity; you will be leading and following others during a scene just as much as you did in these exercises. Here's another exercise exploring this through sound (see Figure 4.4).

EXERCISE 4.7   COOKIE SEARCH

1. Everyone in the group chooses a partner. Then the entire group stands together in a clump at the center of the room with eyes closed. Then all spin around a few times until no one knows which way he or she is facing.

2. Without opening your eyes, move slowly in whatever direction you are facing until you reach a wall or other obstacle. Avoid touching anyone else; feel your way with all of your nonvisual senses.

3. When you have gone as far as you can (and still have not opened your eyes), begin to search for your partner using only the word *cookie*.

4. When you find each other, open your eyes and wait in silence for all to finish. Enjoy watching the others search. Feel the drama of the exercise.

In this exercise, you were not led but had to find your own way toward the sounds of your partner. Did you feel lonely while searching for your partner and relieved when you found him or her? Don't be the kind of actor who makes partners feel lonely during a performance!

Seeing and Hearing

The **plot** of a play moves toward a dramatic conclusion as *energy passes from character to character through a series of interactions that form the scenes of the play* (more on this crucial idea later). The continuity and strength of this flow of energy are what give the story its momentum, which in acting we call **pace**. If

FIGURE 4.4
A Cookie Search

the flow is interrupted for any reason, the momentum is broken, and the evolving drama stalls, causing a drop in dramatic tension and suspense.

Actors usually focus their attention on the energy they *send* to another actor as they pursue their objectives through the actions of their characters. It is equally important, however, that each actor *receive* the energy from the other actors, which provokes each action (again, more on this in later steps.). This is why we say that *acting is reacting.*

Actors receive energy, of course, through seeing and hearing one another. Moreover, drama involves circumstances in which what the characters get from one another has special significance; seeing and hearing on stage must therefore be more acute than in real life. It is also important that the actors receive and give real energies in the present moment. If actors react only to their premeditated ideas of what they are "supposed" to be receiving from another actor, instead of what they are really receiving here and now, the flow of the scene will not be a real human event.

One way to experience such heightened perception is to think of yourself as a camera that is recording everything you see and hear on stage. This is not just a metaphor; an audience does, in fact, tend to mimic the seeing and hearing of the actor. When you focus intently on a particular detail on stage, for example, audience members feel as if they are seeing that detail in a "close-up." You act as a virtual camera for your audience. Here is an enjoyable exercise that will give you the experience of this kind of significant seeing and hearing.

EXERCISE 4.8   CAMERA GAME

Choose some simple activity that you can do with a partner, such as playing a game of cards, preparing a meal, bowling, or playing tennis. You and your partner should take turns being the "camera." Whoever is the camera should take the most interesting pictures possible; you are free to move in any way the camera might move, zooming in for close-ups, panning across the scene, cutting from one angle to another, and so on. When your teacher or your partner randomly calls out "Switch," you will instantly switch roles between camera and subject.

After the exercise, discuss the scene. Was your hearing and seeing of one another heightened? Did being the camera give you greater freedom from self-awareness? Were you more active as the camera? Do you see why having a meaningful and active objective (in this case taking pictures) is so effective on stage?

Summary of Step 4

Actors always work in a group situation. The success of the process depends on the ability of everyone to work together toward the common goal of bringing the material to life. When a group works together in the best possible way, the energy of each member of the group flows into a common stream, forming one energy that is greater than the sum of its parts. Such ideal teamwork is achieved only when five conditions have been met: First, each member is genuinely committed to being a member of the team; second, each member supports the work of the others; third, that support is founded on trust and mutual respect; fourth, all agree to maintain free and open communication; and fifth, the efforts of each member are aligned with the common purpose. When all these conditions have been met, each member of the group is empowered to do his or her best work and each gets more energy from the group than he or she gives to it.

The connection between actors, through which the energy of the scene flows, depends on the ability of each actor to lead and to follow simultaneously, and to give and receive through significant hearing, seeing, and touching. The real interactions between actors, when created in this way, provide a strong focus of attention that helps to reduce self-awareness and thereby promotes creativity.

PART TWO

Action and Character

Consider the word "actor." At its root, it means "someone who *does* something." Think for a moment: Why do you do things in everyday life? Usually, it is to get something you want or need. Sometimes what you need is related to physical survival: food, money, or shelter. Sometimes your need is emotional: to be understood, to be loved, to find peace or beauty. Whatever your need, if it is urgent enough, you *do* something about it. You *act* in order to achieve some **objective** that you hope will satisfy your **need**.

Characters in plays, TV shows, and movies are shown in situations in which something important is happening. In such dramatic situations, whether funny or sad, the needs of the characters are heightened; they are compelled to try to satisfy their needs by doing extraordinary things. This is what makes the story interesting to us; we feel **suspense** as we wait to see whether the characters will get what they need or not. Will Oedipus find the killer of Laius? Will Romeo and Juliet get together? Will Spiderman save the world? We feel involved in the action because it is easy to put ourselves in the place of the characters; like them, we also try to do things to fulfill our needs every day, though not usually in such extraordinary ways or circumstances. This view of acting as "doing" rather than "showing" or "telling about" is the single most important concept in the contemporary view of the actor's art. It is summed up by the term **action**, and you cannot understand the modern idea of acting without understanding the idea of action.

This basic definition of acting is at the heart of everything in this book: *Immediate and urgent needs cause actions in the pursuit of objectives within given circumstances.* This is a complex idea; read it aloud several times, and become aware of each of its four elements: *needs, actions, objectives*, and *circumstances*. We will explore each of these elements here in Part 2.

Example Plays

As the remaining steps examine each component of the acting process, I will provide examples taken from three plays: Arthur Miller's *Death of a Salesman*, Tennessee Williams's *The Glass Menagerie*, and Lorraine Hansberry's *A Raisin in the Sun*. My examples will be much more useful to you if you read these plays in their entirety at the outset. They are available in libraries and bookstores, in paperback, and in many anthologies. All these plays were also produced as feature films and are available on video. Several versions of *Death of a Salesman* include a 1951 feature starring Fredric March, a 1966 version with the original Willy, Lee J. Cobb, and a 1985 production with Dustin Hoffman. The best of several film versions of *The Glass Menagerie* was made in 1987, was directed by Paul Newman, and starred Joanne Woodward and John Malkovich. *A Raisin in the Sun* was filmed in 1961 and starred Sidney Poitier, Ruby Dee, and Claudia McNeil. (A 1989 version with Danny Glover and Esther Rolle gives a good sense of how the play lived on stage.) Watching any of these films will enhance the experience of reading the play but will not substitute for it.

Selecting Your Scene

In the steps that follow, you will apply the concepts presented to a scene from a play that you and one of your fellow students will develop throughout the remainder of this book. Step by step, you will develop the scene in the same way you would in a normal rehearsal process. Here in Part 2, you will begin by understanding the specifics provided by the text, then explore the action of the scene and the internal processes that drive it, and then begin to develop your character. In Part 3, you will extend your character work, and then finally stage the scene and perform it.

It is important that you choose this scene carefully. Once you have teamed up with a partner from your class, work together to choose a two-character scene that will serve you both well. Since at this beginning stage of your development as an actor you don't want to burden yourself with advanced technical problems, keep the following qualities in mind when selecting your scene:

1. Choose a *realistic* and *contemporary* scene, written in language that is comfortable for you.
2. Make sure the characters are *close to you* in age.
3. Choose a *short* scene that can be read aloud in no more than three to five minutes (or if necessary, a smaller section of a longer scene).
4. Most important, select a scene that *touches* you personally in some way.

A list of useful plays and scene anthologies appears in Appendix B. Whatever the source of your scene, it is very important that you read the entire play from which the scene comes. Only in this way can you come to understand how your character and the scene itself functions within the story as a whole; this understanding is necessary to guide the many choices you will make as you develop the scene.

STEP 5

Exploring the Text

Your work begins with the words provided by the playwright, and your first task is to understand those words and to respond to them as fully as possible. One of the first things you will notice about a well-written play is how its language expresses the feelings and personalities of the characters. Unlike any other kind of writing, the words of a play are intended to be spoken aloud, and a good playwright writes not for a silent reader, but for you, the actor. The way those words will affect you when you speak them is a major concern of the writer's, and he or she has supplied words that impart not only information, but also emotions and sensations through their rhythms, sounds, and structure.

The words your character speaks are determined by the writer's vision of your character's mind, body, desires, and feelings. If you let those words come into you and participate in them actively, you can begin to enter into the character. As we mentioned in Step 3, the old-fashioned acting adage, "Just say the words," had some truth to it, though only if the words are said with a full re-creation of the living psychological and physical condition that produces them. Your study of your role, therefore, begins with respect for the details and implications of your character's language, which has been so carefully wrought by the author to serve you.

In Step 3 you experienced how, in everyday life, speech is the result of a process; you begin with a *germinal* idea or feeling, an impulse that needs to be formed into words, and you then choose the words that will best communicate to others. Although this *process of verbalization* usually happens almost instantaneously, complex thoughts and deep feelings sometimes require considerable effort to put into words. A dramatic character on stage must go through this same process of verbalization, and you, the actor playing the character, must re-create and reexperience this process each and every time you speak your lines. This is the only way to keep your character's language alive, happening right now, "as if before our eyes." If you fail to relive this process of word choice, your lines will inevitably sound mechanical and rehearsed. As good actors say, you must come to "own" the character's words as if they were your own by re-creating and reexperiencing the living process by which that language is formed. This requires working backward from the finished language provided by the writer to discover its genesis in the mind of the character. In this step, you will explore the clues within the character's language that can lead you to direct participation in the mind and body that produces that language.

Word Choice

The critical moment in the process of verbalization occurs when characters choose the words they speak in order to communicate an idea or feeling. This word choice is called *diction* (a word sometimes used to mean "enunciation" but used here in its primary meaning, "choice of words to express ideas," as in *dictionary*). The words your character speaks have two kinds of meaning: their literal dictionary meanings, called **denotation**, and their implied emotional values, called **connotation**. We will consider denotation first.

Denotation

The first step toward full participation in your character's language is to be sure you understand the literal meaning of the words he or she speaks. Some of the words may be unusual, tied to a specific time and place, or simply unknown to you. There may be several possible definitions for a word and you will need to understand meaning within the particular context of the character. Moreover, denotation is not a static thing and the meaning of words in popular usage sometimes changes quickly. You must be sure that the meaning you take for granted today is not a distortion of the playwright's original intention.

This is a particular problem when dealing with older plays. For example, Juliet, coming out on her balcony, says, "O Romeo, Romeo! Wherefore art thou Romeo?" Some young actresses deliver this line as if Juliet were wishing that Romeo were there, in the sense of "Romeo, where are you?" But when we discover that in Shakespeare's day *wherefore* meant "why," we see that she really is saying, "Why are you named Romeo, member of a family hated by my own?" Such obsolete meanings are sometimes labeled "archaic" in the dictionary.

Even more recent plays may use words or phrases whose meaning is obscure, or has changed in common usage, is involved in particular activities, or is tied to a particular social or economic class. *The Glass Menagerie* is full of references to things like Guernica, blanc mange, the Midas touch, Gay Deceivers, and other references that will need to be understood. *Raisin in the Sun* has many terms that are particular to the social, racial, and ethnic classes represented. Even very recent plays like *Clybourne Park* and *Red* may require some research.

Playwrights will sometimes manipulate denotation by *punning*, placing a word that has more than one denotation in a context in which both meanings could be applied. Although puns have been called the lowest form of humor, they may be used for both serious and comic effects. For example, when we examine the names of Beckett's characters in his play *Endgame*, we see that the name of the master "Hamm" reminds us of meat, while his servant "Clov" refers to the spice (clove) traditionally used with ham for flavor and preservation. But Beckett doesn't stop there; ham is meat that comes from an animal with a cloven hoof, and Clov does indeed act as the "feet" of Hamm, since Hamm cannot walk. There is also the "Ham actor," the tragedian, and Clov, the clown; and the overbearing Hamm (hammer) pounds down Clov *(clou* means "nail" in French) as well as the other two characters in the play, Nagg and Nell *(nagel* means "nail" in German). All these multiple meanings are wonderfully appropriate to the play and demonstrate how much meaning can be achieved despite the highly condensed nature of a play's dialogue.

Characters in plays frequently use topical and *colloquial* speech, the highly informal, conversational language of a particular time and place. For example, calling a beautiful woman "a dish" or "a real tomato," or her legs "a pair of gams," summons up 1930s' America in a very specific way. Colloquial words and phrases tend to change their meaning very quickly, and doing a play even ten years old may require some investigation of the meaning of words and expressions it contains.

Good dictionaries will help you to be sure about denotation. For old plays, the *Oxford English Dictionary* (OED) lists the changing meanings of words with the dates of their currency. There are also carefully noted editions of great classical plays with glossaries and notes that are very helpful. For more recent plays, there are slang dictionaries available, and general dictionaries like *The American Heritage dictionary* can help keep you up to date.

Connotation

Whereas denotation refers to the literal meaning of words, *connotation* is defined as "suggestive or associative implication of a term beyond its literal, explicit sense." The connotation of words can reveal the attitudes and feelings of a character. A dictionary will sometimes be helpful in giving examples of connotations, but the connotative possibilities of words are multiple and variable. You need to consider the context in order to determine which of the connotative possibilities of a word are appropriate. The word "politic," for example, is defined as "artful; ingenious; shrewd" but also as "crafty; unscrupulous; cunning." When Shakespeare's King Lear speaks of "a scurvy politician," we know that he intends the latter meanings. Likewise, when Blanche DuBois in

A Streetcar Named Desire describes Stanley Kowalski as "swilling and gnawing and hulking," we understand not only her attitude toward Stanley but also something about Blanche herself because she has chosen to express her disgust in such vividly bodily ways. The physical qualities of "swilling and gnawing and hulking" invite the actress to participate in the sensations they evoke, and this physicalization of the language can provide a strong sense of not only Blanche's disgust for Stanley but also her barely suppressed sexuality.

To sum up, your understanding of your lines depends on your understanding of their meaning and feeling in a historical, social, and psychological context. You must consider *the meanings of the words when the play was written* and *the feelings they express when used by this kind of character in this situation.* One very good way to be sure you have examined the meanings of your lines is to **paraphrase** the lines, restating them in your own words as if you were doing a translation of the original. Obviously, much of the emotional tone and poetic richness of the original will be lost, but you will have ensured that you have considered seriously the possible values of each word you speak.

> EXERCISE 5.1   **PARAPHRASE ON THREE LEVELS**
>
> Using one of the more important speeches from your scene, write a paraphrase of it on each of the following levels:
>
> 1. To express as simply as possible the *germinal idea* behind each sentence
> 2. To express the literal denotation, word by word
> 3. To express the connotations and emotional attitudes by pushing the feelings to an extreme, using language that is natural to you
> 4. Read this last paraphrase aloud, trying to express the intention of the original.

Rhythm

The rhythm of speech refers to its tempo (fast or slow), its underlying "beat" (regular or irregular, heavy or light), and the variations of tempo and beat that provide emphasis on certain words or other elements of the speech, thereby enhancing their meaning. Rhythm is highly expressive of personality; a blustery, pompous person has a rhythm of speech much different from a thoughtful, introspective person. Even nationality and social background affect rhythm; the Irish, for example, tend to speak each thought on one long exhalation of breath, imparting an unmistakable rhythm to their speech. Good playwrights build in the rhythms of speech that are appropriate to a character's personality, background, and emotion, and your analysis of those rhythms will aid you in forming your characterization.

Many emotions have recognizable rhythmic implications. All emotions cause measurable changes in the tension of our muscles, and this tensing of the muscles has a direct effect on our speech. Take anger as an example: As anger rises in us, the body becomes tense, especially in the deep center, where our largest muscles mobilize themselves for action. This tension in the interior muscles is communicated directly to the diaphragm, limiting its movement and forcing us to take shallow breaths; but since we need to oxygenate our muscles for defense purposes, we compensate by taking more rapid breaths. These changes cause us to break up our speech into shorter breath phrases and to increase its tempo. Tension spreading to the pharynx causes an elevation of pitch, which, when coupled with the increased pressure of the breath stream, results in a "punching" delivery and increased volume. As the tension moves into the jaw, it encourages us to emphasize hard consonant sounds. As a result, our angry speech may become similar to the snapping and growling of an animal about to bite. (Charles Darwin, in a section of his theory of evolution, suggested that all human emotions are expressed by vestiges of animal behavior that were once practical, like biting, but have now become symbolic.)

This very basic example shows you that both rhythm and tone are tied to your emotional state by the muscles that produce speech. Playwrights write with a special sensitivity to the way the words will feel when spoken by an actor; by understanding the rhythms and tones your playwright has supplied for you, and by experiencing them in your own muscles as you pronounce the words, you will have a chance to experience the feelings they express.

A skillful writer shapes rhythm on several levels at once. The fundamental rhythm is established by the flow of accented and unaccented syllables; we call this the **syllable cadence.** Look at the following example from Samuel Beckett's *Endgame*; you will see that Beckett has used rhythmic patterns of two and three syllables. Read the passage aloud for full rhythmic effect; tap your feet.

> One day you'll be blind, like me. You'll be sitting there, a speck in the void, in the dark, forever, like me. (pause) One day you'll say to yourself, I'm tired. I'll sit down, and you'll go and sit down. Then you'll say, I'm hungry, I'll get up and get something to eat. But you won't get up. You'll say, I shouldn't have sat down, but since I have I'll sit on a little longer, then I'll get up and get something to eat. But you won't get up and you won't get anything to eat. (*Pause*) You'll look at the wall a while, then you'll say, I'll close my eyes, perhaps have a little sleep, after that I'll feel better, and you'll close them. And when you open them again there'll be no wall anymore. (Pause) Infinite emptiness will be all around you, all the resurrected dead of all the ages wouldn't fill it, and there you'll be, like a little bit of grit, in the middle of the steppe.

The rhythmic flow of these syllables is as highly developed as any formal poetry.

Another level of rhythm, the **breath cadence,** is of special importance to an actor. The evolution of our written language was greatly influenced by the physical act of speaking; we tend to divide our thoughts into sentences that can be said in one breath. When a thought is complex enough to require several phrases, we separate these into "subbreaths" by commas, semicolons, or colons (in music the comma is still used as a breath mark). Playwrights manipulate breath cadences to guide an actor into a pattern of breathing, and the rhythm of breath is a primary factor in emotion. Try reading the Beckett piece aloud, taking a small breath at every comma, a full breath at each period, and a long breath at each "(pause)." What emotional experience results? Next, try the same experiment using the speech from your scene which you paraphrased in Exercise 5.1.

Finally, the dialogue itself, as the characters speak one after another, has a rhythm. Each speech usually contains a central idea and functions in a way similar to that of paragraphs in prose; the alternation of the speeches creates the **dialogue cadence**. We get a good impression of the tempo of a scene by looking at the density of the printed script; a mass of long speeches suggests a different approach to tempo, for example, than does an extremely short back-and-forth exchange. You may notice, too, that changes in tempo and rhythm are suggested by a sudden change in the dialogue cadence, as when one character's very long speech is answered by a short response from the other, or when a scene breaks into a series of very short exchanges of shared or interrupted lines, which in classical drama is called **stichomythia**.

Here is a summary of these cadences, or levels of rhythm:

1. Syllable cadence
2. Breath cadence
3. Dialogue cadence

As useful and evocative as the rhythm of your speech is, rhythm does not absolutely determine meaning or even emotion; your choices about delivering your lines must be based upon your understanding of the meaning of the lines within the demands of character and situation. Nevertheless, by recognizing the rhythms and sounds the writer has built into your character's speech, and by experiencing them fully in your own muscles, you will find them a powerful aid in entering into the consciousness of your character. As Stanislavski said:

> There is an indissoluble interdependence, interaction and bond between tempo-rhythm and feeling....The correctly established tempo-rhythm of a play or a role can, of itself, intuitively (on occasion automatically) take hold of the feelings of an actor and arouse in him a true sense of living his part.[1]

EXERCISE 5.2   **THE RHYTHMS OF THE SCENE**

Using the same speech you chose for your paraphrase (Exercise 5.1), with your partner examine your scene as a whole. Does the dialogue cadence give you any clues about the way the scene should flow? Together, create a musical dance of the entire scene, perhaps throwing a ball back and forth between you as the dialogue flows.

The Music of Speech

There is a story about the famous Italian actress Eleanora Duse. Her speech, it was said, was so emotionally rich that she once moved a New York audience to tears by reading from the Manhattan telephone book. True or not, the story shows that any good actor develops great expressiveness in the use of the music

---

[1]From Constantin Stanislavski, *Building a Character*, trans. Elizabeth Reynolds Hapgood (New York: Theater Arts Books, 1949), pp. 218–236. Theater Arts Books, 153 Waverly Place, New York, NY 10014.

of speech, and playwrights are careful to provide language that is rich in its musical potential, whatever other qualities it may have, from the lyrical sweep of Tennessee Williams to the curt staccato of David Mamet.

There have been attempts to develop systems that attach certain meanings to certain linguistic sounds. The most famous of these was the **Roback Voco-Sensory Theory**. In one of his experiments, Roback's subjects were asked to tell which three-letter nonsense syllable, "mil" or "mal," made them think of larger or smaller objects. As you might guess, most subjects thought that "mal" meant something bigger than "mil." The theory points out that the physical act of saying "mal" requires opening the mouth more than does saying "mil," and this causes the sensation of bigness associated with "mal." The opposite is true for "mil," which is a "smaller" sound. The theory goes on to suggest that much of language was formed by the effect of the physical sensations of speaking: Rough words *feel* rough, and smooth words *feel* smooth, for example, just as *rushing* rushes, *explodes* explodes, and so on.

This theory has great limitations, however, since many words do not seem to relate to their physical qualities; for instance, *small* is made up of big sounds, while *big* has small sounds. Nevertheless, the theory provides an interesting view of language for an actor since it encourages a way of speaking that emphasizes the relationship of physical sensation and the meaning and feeling of speech. Try reading again the previous speech from Samuel Beckett's *Endgame* (see page 50) so as to emphasize its tonal values. Feel how Beckett has selected words whose sounds can be useful to you in supporting the meaning and emotional tone of the speech. Feel especially the shift from big, open vowel sounds in the main body of the speech, in lines like "infinite emptiness will be all around you," to the little, hard consonant sounds in the last line, "And there you'll be, like a little bit of grit, in the middle of the steppe." Do you see how this shift can communicate a vivid experience of the isolation and insignificance the speaker feels?

Stanislavski, in *Building a Character*, sums it up this way:

> Letters, syllables, words—these are the musical notes of speech, out of which we fashion measures, arias, whole symphonies. There is good reason to describe beautiful speech as musical....Musical speech opens up endless possibilities of conveying the inner life of a role.[2]

Tone and rhythm give our speech color and individual flavor and make it fully human. Through careful and informed analysis of your lines, you can unlock these inherent values of tone and rhythm, and by surrendering yourself to the muscular actions required to produce them, you can bring them back to life for your audience and, more importantly, for yourself. In this way, the music of your character's speech can help you to enter actively into the life of the role.

---

[2]From Constantin Stanislavski, *Building a Character,* trans. Elizabeth Reynolds Hapgood (New York: Theater Arts Books, 1949), pp. 218–236. Theater Arts Books, 153 Waverly Place, New York, NY 10014.

EXERCISE 5.3 **THE MUSIC OF SPEECH**

Using the same speech you chose for your paraphrase (Exercise 5.1), analyze its rhythmic and tonal qualities. Use markings, colored pencils, or other devices to help you recognize the rhythmic and tonal patterns in the speech.

1. Using large bodily movements and nonverbal sound, create a "musical dance" of the speech that exaggerates its rhythmic and tonal patterns. Move from your deep center, and involve your breath.
2. Then immediately read the speech as written, but this time speak the words without moving. See how much of your body's memory of the first version carries over to enrich the speech as your deep muscles continue to respond to it even without external movement.

The Given Circumstances

Besides the meanings and music of the characters' speech, there is another kind of essential information provided by the text of a play, and that is a sense of the world in which the characters live, and the nature of the relationships between them. The specific qualities of the character's world and relationships are called the *given circumstances*, or the **givens** for short. These are important because a character lives only in relation to his or her world and the other characters within it.

Psychologists say that personality is shaped by both nature and nurture. Think of the ways your own personality has been shaped both by your genetic inheritance (your nature) and by the world in which you grew up (your nurture). Every day you interact with your world. It has physical, psychological, and social aspects that profoundly influence your feelings and thoughts. In reaction to these experiences, your personality is continuing to change and evolve in the direction established by your nature.

A character in a play has been given a nature by the author, who may even tell us something of the character's personal background prior to the beginning of the play—commonly called the character's **backstory**. But the character is also expressed by nurture, by his or her interaction with the other characters in the play, and by the world created by the author, a world created specifically to serve the story. As an actor, then, you must not only work on the inner qualities of your character but also strive to experience the character's world and let your characterization develop within it.

The givens fall into three categories: *who*, *where*, and *when*. Let's briefly examine each.

Who

Because personality is formed and influenced by our interactions with those around us, your character can be fully understood only by examining the *relationships* between him or her and all the other characters, including those who may not be on stage in the scene you have selected. These relationships have two aspects: the *general* and the *specific*. The general relationship provides basic considerations that make a relationship similar to others of its kind, whereas the specific relationship reveals what is unique to this particular case.

For example, in *Death of a Salesman*, Willy has a general relationship with his neighbor Charley. Like many neighbors, they talk about their work and their families and even give each other advice. But Willy and Charley also have a specific relationship that is very important to the overall meaning of the play. Charley is an easygoing man who, unlike Willy, has strong self-esteem. Charley advises Willy to accept himself and his life and be thankful for all he has. He even offers Willy a job, one that Willy's pride will not allow him to accept. In all, Charley represents a worldview that, if Willy could adopt it, might save his life.

Charley is sharply contrasted with Willy's brother Ben, who lives like a ghost in Willy's mind. Ben is the ultimate embodiment of the American Dream. Like the popular folk hero Horatio Alger, he tells Willy to "go West" and seek his fortune. One of the most important scenes in the play occurs when Willy is playing cards with Charley while at the same time talking to the image of Ben. This scene shows us Willy being torn between the two ways of life embodied by Charley and Ben, neither of which he can really accept because of his deep-seated insecurity. At the end of the play, we see the contrast between Charley and Ben carried on in Willy's sons: Happy sounds like Willy when he declares, "He had a good dream. It's the only dream you can have—to come out number-one man," but Biff sounds more like Charley when he answers, "I know who I am, kid."

Although there is usually a great deal of information about major characters and their relationships, minor characters, like Bobo in *A Raisin in the Sun* or Bernard in *Death of a Salesman* are usually given virtually no history and limited delineation. We might know only that one is a small, frightened, unsuccessful businessman and the other a serious, intelligent, and ultimately successful man. Minor characters most often serve to reveal some aspect of the major characters; Bobo shows us the foolishness of Walter's plans, and Bernard shows us how the values of his father Charley have resulted in happiness and success. It is up to the actors playing such characters to flesh them out in a way that is interesting, believable, and most of all appropriate to their function within the play as a whole, and with a sense of economy that does not distract from the main story.

Where

Where the play happens has two main aspects: the physical and the social. The *physical* environment has a tremendous influence on the action. For example, Shakespeare chose to set a play of great passion, *Othello*, in the hot and humid climate of Cyprus, whereas his play of intrigue and indecision, *Hamlet*, is properly set in the cold and isolated climate of Denmark. Likewise, the urban setting and the terribly cramped quarters of the apartments in *A Raisin in the Sun* and

The Glass Menagerie embody Walter's and Tom's feelings of being trapped in a life over which they have no control.

The *social* environment is also of great importance and needs to be understood in terms of the values at the time the play is set. Our credit card culture, for example, cannot fully appreciate the importance to Willy Loman of "weathering a 20-year mortgage," or the humiliation of Amanda Wingfield in having to ask Garfinkle's Delicatessen for credit. The idea of "the American Dream" is tremendously important in *A Raisin in the Sun* and *Death of a Salesman*, and the longing of people to rise within society drives both.

When

When a scene is happening is important in terms of the *time of day* and the *season*. *Death of a Salesman* begins in the summer—the season of warmth, growth, and fulfillment—and ends in the fall—the season of cold, decay, and impending death.

The *historical period* of a play—with all its implications for manners, values, and beliefs—is another important aspect of "when." Most of *The Glass Menagerie* is a memory of the 1930s, before World War II, and Tom tells us in his first speech that the Great Depression and "labor disturbances" at home and civil unrest overseas are "the social background of the play." *A Raisin in the Sun* is set in the years after World War II, when many African American men returned from the war and an integrated army only to find that racism still oppressed them at home.

Remember too that your character is a creature of the theater and it will be useful for you to understand the theatrical world for which he or she was created. Reading other plays by your author and his or her contemporaries can help; so can study of the physical and social environment of the theater of the time. For instance, the open-air, thrust quality of the Elizabethan playhouse with its pit in which the "groundlings" stood throughout the performance is important to an understanding of Shakespeare's plays. Just so, it is revealing to learn that the Moscow Art Theater in which Chekhov's plays were first presented sat 1,200 persons, so that the scale of the performances must have been somewhat larger than we usually think.

Likewise, try to understand the literary conventions that influenced the writer; it is revealing to learn of Chekhov's passion for the writing of the French Naturalists and their "scientific" approach to behavior; this is even more illuminating when we consider his training as a doctor and the fact that he wrote his four great plays after learning that he was dying of tuberculosis. In the same way, understanding the writer's psychological and moral values can be revealing; it is helpful to know that Bertolt Brecht was an ambulance driver in World War I and was permanently affected by the carnage he experienced.

Older plays, or plays set in the past or other cultures, may present givens that are foreign to you, and some research will be required. In period plays, knowledge of the history, architecture, painting, music, religion, politics, and fashion of the time can be very useful.

To sum up, here is a list of the givens:

1. Who
   a. General relationships
   b. Specific relationships
2. Where
   a. Physical environment
   b. Social environment
3. When
   a. Time of day
   b. Season
   c. Historical period

Each of these given circumstances must be evaluated as to its relative importance; don't waste thought and energy on aspects of a character's world that do not contribute to the action and meaning of the play.

When possible, actually experiencing the most important givens can be a great help in rehearsing a scene. Consider working in locations that approximate the conditions of the scene. For example, rehearsing Shakespeare's *A Midsummer Night's Dream* in the woods at night by lantern light can create an experience that may greatly enrich the stage performance. In the same way, rehearsing *The Glass Menagerie* or *A Raisin in the Sun* in a cramped space may help to instill a sense of the oppression the character's feel.

A note of caution: Beginning actors sometimes try to "indicate" the givens. Remember that it is not your job to *show* the audience anything about the character's world. Your job is simply to *live* in that world and let it affect you.

EXERCISE 5.4 **THE GIVENS**

1. Working with your partner, analyze the given circumstances of your scene, and discuss the influence of each on your character and on the action.
2. Rehearse the scene in ways that help you to experience the influence of the givens. For example, you might rehearse in a place that provides similar physical conditions to those of the play.
3. Carrying your script in hand if necessary, perform your scene for your group. Try to experience the givens as fully as possible.
4. Afterward, discuss with the group the sense of the givens they got from your performance and the influence of the givens on the scene. Did you avoid indicating the givens?

Summary of Step 5

When you set out to create a role, you necessarily begin with the character's language. You must come to "own" these words as if they were your own by re-creating and reexperiencing the living process by which that language is formed. This requires working backward from the finished language provided by the writer to discover its genesis in the mind of the character.

The words your character speaks have two kinds of meaning: their diction-ary meanings, called denotation, and their emotional values, called connotation. While denotation refers to the literal meaning of words, connotation can reveal the attitudes and feelings of a character. You must consider the meanings of the words when the play was written and the feelings the words express when used by this kind of character in this situation. One way to be sure you have exam-ined the meanings of your lines is to paraphrase them, to restate them in your own words.

Good playwrights build in the rhythms and tonality of speech that are appropriate to a character's personality and emotion. The character's language is tied to your emotional state by the muscular activity that produces speech; an active physical participation in your character's language is a powerful tool for enter-ing into the character's mind.

A character is created in relationship to other characters and within a par-ticular world. These given circumstances (who, where, and when) are essential to a proper understanding and experience of the character. It will also be use-ful for you to understand the theatrical world for which your character was created.

STEP 6

Objectives and Actions

LEARNING OBJECTIVES

- Discover the central concept of action as it is used by the effective actor.
- Experience how your character's *need* generates an *objective* (what he or she wants) and drives him or her to commit an *action* in pursuit of this objective.
- Distinguish how this dramatic action is based upon and yet differs from action in everyday life.
- Compare the various implications of Stanislavski's use of this idea as related to concepts like public solitude, dual consciousness, the relationship of emotion and action, and the qualities of automatic (or habitual) actions.
- Explore the qualities that render actions useful for stage purposes and how counteractions heighten dramatic tension.
- Experience how objectives hidden beneath the surface of your character's behavior (subtext) enrich your performance.

In order to begin understanding the concept of action, we have to go all the way back to 350 BCE and the very first writing about Western drama, Aristotle's *Poetics*. The main difference between plays and other kinds of writing, Aristotle said, is that plays show us things happening *as if before our eyes* and *for the first time*. Other kinds of writing can tell us a story and may even contain dramatic elements, but a play presents the story as something happening right now, right here. A play is not "about" something; it "is" the event itself.

In the same way, the good actor's performance is not "about" the character; it "is" the character living before our eyes. Consequently, we say that acting is *doing*, not showing or telling. Like the play itself, the actor has to be here and now, doing the thing itself as if for the first time, *in action*.

For the actor, action is whatever the character does to try to achieve an objective. Action may take many forms: physical, vocal, intellectual, emotional, and spiritual. When an actor is truly in action, all these aspects of the performance become interconnected: An adjustment in the body can generate a change of emotion, a change in the voice can generate new thoughts and emotions, a new emotional experience can generate physical and vocal changes, and so on. Acting can be approached in all of these ways, and the best actor training programs simultaneously address them all. This explains why so many different acting techniques can all produce good results, though one or another may be more effective for an individual actor.

Whether they approach acting primarily through the body and voice, the mind, the emotions, or the spirit, all contemporary acting techniques are aimed at creating a dynamic actor who does things in a total, authentic, and dramatically effective way, rather than an actor who merely shows us an image or idea of the character instead of the living character in action.

Stanislavski's View of Action

The great Russian director Constantin Stanislavski (1863–1938) was one of the first to explore this idea of action in a systematic way. He was dissatisfied with the overblown acting style of his time; too often, he felt, the actor's display of emotion and technique became an end in itself and overshadowed the meaning of the play. Stanislavski set out to create a new system of acting aimed at economy, greater psychological truthfulness, and, above all, respect for the meaning of the play. He based his system on the idea that everything an actor does in a performance has to be connected to the character's internal need. As Stanislavski said:

> There are no physical actions divorced from some desire, some effort in some direction, some objective.... Everything that happens on the stage has a definite purpose.[1]

He called this **justification**. According to the principle of justification, everything the actor does as the character should grow directly out of the needs of the character and be directed toward some objective. In this way, the "inner" world of the character and the "outer" world of the performance are unified, two sides of the same coin. This is what Stanislavski called a "truthful" performance, and this book is based on Stanislavski's idea. Specifically, at each moment of the performance, your character wants something (your *need*), which makes you do something (your *action*) in an effort to achieve a desired goal (your *objective*). (Some schools of acting use the terms "intention" or "task" instead of "objective," but they all mean the same thing.)

To put it even more simply; *need causes an action directed toward an objective.* We will explore each element of this central idea in later steps. Read this central idea aloud several times, and feel the *flow* of energy from *need* to *action* toward *objective.*

---

[1]Constantin Stanislavski, *An Actor's Handbook,* trans. and ed. Elizabeth Reynolds Hapgood (New York: Theatre Arts Books, 1936), p. 8. Copyright © 1936, 1961, 1963 by Elizabeth Reynolds Hapgood.

Constantin Stanislvaksy

The power of this approach is that because your attention, in rehearsal and performance, is focused on the character's objective, you gain concentration, relaxation, economy, spontaneity, and reduction in self-awareness. Best of all, however, this focus helps to put you *into* your character in an active way: You *want* what the character wants in his or her circumstances, and you *do* what the character does to try to get it. This gives you a living experience of the character and leads to what Stanislavski called **transformation** as you become a new version of yourself; this new version of yourself is the created character, which—as Stanislavski said—is a marriage of the actor and the role.

It is important to understand that for Stanislavski action was not just external activity. A cat watching a mouse hole is not moving at all, yet we recognize the drama of the action that the cat's objectives might produce. Action, therefore, is felt even before it has shown itself in external activity; it lives even in the *potential* for doing. At such moments, the **inner action** is living inside us, waiting to erupt into the outside world. Stanislavski called this inner action **spiritual action** and the outer action it produces *physical action:*

The creation of the physical life is half the work on a role because, like us, a role has two natures, physical and spiritual.... a role on the stage, more than action in real life, must bring together the two lives—of external and internal action—in mutual effort to achieve a given purpose.[2]

Both internal and external actions are essential, as Stanislavski pointed out:

External action acquires inner meaning and warmth from inner action, while [inner action] finds its expression only in physical terms.[3]

If your action consists only of external movement and speech unconnected to an inner energy, it will seem hollow and lifeless. But if your action lives only as inner intensity, without skillful outer expression, it will seem vague and self-indulgent. The most useful approach, then, is to avoid thinking of inner and outer actions as being in any way separate. Imagine instead *a single flow of action that has both an inner phase and an outer phase.*

Action and Emotion

Although emotion will eventually be an important part of a performance, a good actor does not begin working on emotions themselves. Genuine and specific emotion is achieved—on stage as in life—only as the *result* of action, of trying to do something important. Think of something you want desperately: If you get it, you are happy; if you don't, you are sad. If you don't get what you want and it is not your fault, you feel angry; when you don't get what you want and you don't know why, you feel afraid or frustrated. In all these cases, you act on your need first, and emotion follows; so it should be in performance. *Action produces emotion, not the other way around.*

Some actors think that they must *feel* something before they *do* anything. You sometimes hear them say, "I don't feel it yet." Of course you want to find the emotional state of your character so that your actions will have the proper quality and tone, but finding the right emotion is a *process* of trial and error, and the emotion is the *result* of the process, not its starting point. You must *do* before you can *feel*. Even if a script gives you an indication of your character's emotional condition in a scene, you should not play that emotion; rather you will find it by experiencing the character's action while pursuing his or her objective in a way that results in the correct emotion.

Trying to generate an emotion as the basis for action is an unreliable and exhausting method and may or may not produce stageworthy results. The play gives us actions: words to say and things to do. It makes sense to begin our work with the action the writer has provided, and use it to lead us to the psychological and spiritual conditions that it evokes in us when we fully commit ourselves

---

[2]Constantin Stanislavski, *Building a Character*, trans. Elizabeth Reynolds Hapgood (New York: Theatre Arts Books, 1949), pp. 218–236. Theatre Arts Books, 153 Waverly Place, New York, NY 10014.

[3]Constantin *An Actor's Handbook*, p. 9.

to it. Trying to shortcut this process, to create an emotion for its own sake, is mere trickery lacking in truth for both actor and audience.

Action and Public Solitude

Stanislavski tells of an acting student who, like many of us, suffered from stage fright. The student became tense and distracted on stage because he was overly aware of being watched. One day, his teacher gave him the simple task of counting the floorboards on the stage. The student soon became totally engrossed in this task. When he finished, he realized that it was the first time he had been on stage without self-consciousness. Surprisingly to him, the experience was liberating and exhilarating. Stanislavski points out that it was the student's total focus on his task that had allowed him to forget about being watched. He was *fully in action* and therefore became unself-conscious.

From this experience, Stanislavski developed his principle of the "dramatic task," or what we now call the *objective*. Instead of counting floorboards, Stanislavski began to teach actors to focus their full awareness on what their character was trying to achieve at any given moment, and this is the way we teach the idea of the objective today.

There are several great benefits of learning to focus on your character's objective: first, being engrossed in the objective greatly reduces your self-consciousness by giving you a point of attention outside yourself; second, it makes your energy flow outward and forward into the scene, producing a more dynamic and effective performance that helps to propel the play; and finally, it helps you to enter into the character actively, wanting what he or she wants and doing what he or she does to try to achieve the objective. As you will see in the following steps, this active participation in the character's life is the basis for bringing about a transformation as you find that version of yourself that will become the created character.

When you are entirely focused on your character's objective you have little awareness left for self-consciousness. You will have achieved the condition Stanislavski called **public solitude**. We can see public solitude in real life: an athlete executing a difficult play, people arguing a deeply felt issue, a student studying for a big test, and lovers wooing. All these people are in public solitude because *they have an objective that is so personally significant that they are totally focused on what they are doing.* The more important the objective, the stronger the action and the more complete the focus, until you become so engrossed in what you are doing that everything else fades from your consciousness. Think back to such a moment in your own life and try to relive it.

It is at such moments of public solitude that self-consciousness and fear are conquered. In this way, the objective serves the actor in the same way that a mantra serves a meditator, as a focus of attention that reduces self-awareness. It has been called "a bone thrown to the barking dog of the ego." Here is a simple exercise to help you begin to experience this focus of attention on an objective.

EXERCISE 6.1   **GUARD AND THIEF**

In this game, you and your partner are both blindfolded, or you can simply keep your eyes closed. One of you is the "guard"; the other is a "thief." The thief has the objective of crossing the room and touching the far wall; the guard has the objective of stopping the thief by touching him or her. When the thief is touched by the guard, he or she "dies." At first, the guard is defensive, reacting to the thief, who tries various strategies to get past the guard; but when the teacher calls, "Attack," the guard goes on the attack and seeks out the thief, who tries to elude capture.

Discuss this exercise. Did you experience the focus and liberation of pursuing an important objective? Did you enjoy the drama of the game that resulted from your competing objectives?

EXERCISE 6.2   **A SIMPLE TASK**

Select a simple physical activity that requires great concentration, such as building a house of cards, counting the floorboards or tiles on the floor, or balancing a stick on your nose. Perform this task in front of your class; can you allow yourself to become so absorbed in it that you "forget" that you are in front of an audience?

Dual Consciousness

There is a danger in public solitude. Some young actors tend to focus so much on the solitude that they begin to ignore the requirements of being in public. They try to achieve some sort of trancelike state in which they lose all sense of performance; but public solitude is not like a trance. Like the athlete, you should remain in control, fully aware of your task, and even though you have "forgotten" about the performance, it will still be in the background of your awareness, however slightly; this awareness is the source of your artistic control.

This, then, is the question: Can you be completely engrossed in the action and world of your character and simultaneously be aware of the demands of performance, making the artistic choices required to express your action in a public form worthy of your audience's attention? This question is answered by your capacity for **dual consciousness**, your ability to function on more than one level of awareness at a time. As one of Stanislavski's students put it after a successful performance:

> I divided myself, as it were, into two personalities. One continued as [the character], the other was an observer [the actor]. Strangely enough this duality not only did not impede, it actually promoted my creative work. It encouraged and lent impetus to it.[4]

---

[4]Ibid.

The two levels of consciousness, then, are that of the *character* pursuing his or her objective and that of the *actor* observing and adjusting the performance for the sake of the spectators.

Different performance situations may require more or less emphasis on one of these levels of consciousness or the other. In some broad forms of comedy, for example, we may allow a bit more of the actor to be present in the performance; this explains why stand-up comedians are often successful in television sitcoms even though they may not be very skillful actors in the traditional sense. In naturalistic stage plays, however, we strive to reduce our actor consciousness to the minimum. For the camera the actor must be completely invisible, leaving only the character behind; in fact, we say that the camera requires "no acting" at all. Even in this case, however, you do not lose your actor consciousness completely; if you did, you would lose also your ability to make artistic choices.

Dual consciousness is really a very natural ability. When you were a child, a puddle easily became a vast ocean, but it didn't need to stop being a puddle. You hadn't learned yet that something isn't supposed to be two different things at once, and that we aren't supposed to be in two different realities at the same time. As an actor, you will have to forget your adult logic and allow yourself to rediscover this childhood ability to make believe, to joyfully enter the world of fantasy.

EXERCISE 6.3　**MAKING BELIEVE**

Repeat the simple task given in Exercise 6.2, but this time give yourself a character and a dramatic situation; if your task was to build a house of cards, perhaps you could be a condemned man about to be executed, waiting for the governor to phone with your pardon. If you were balancing a stick on your nose, perhaps you are on a tight rope a hundred feet in the air and trying to escape from a burning building before the rope disintegrates. See if you can relax and accept the character's reality. Are you able to hold the dual awareness of your character's world and your actor's concerns?

Indicating

Acting students commonly do too much on stage. They are afraid that it is not enough to simply do what their character is doing; they try to embellish, to show us how the character feels, or what kind of person the character is. They posture, exaggerate their emotions, use excessive gestures and facial expressions, or take on a false voice. Their performance is saying something like, "Hey, look at how angry I am," or "Look at what a villain I am."

This excessive behavior is called *indicating*. You are indicating when you are *showing* the audience something about the character instead of simply *doing* what the character does. Actors indicate for various reasons. Some feel unworthy of the audience's attention and think they have to work hard to earn it; some indicate because they are afraid of losing control over the performance.

No matter the reason, indicating spoils the performance for the audience. Your job is to present the truthful evidence of the character's living action and leave the judgment and interpretation of it to the audience. If instead you *show* the audience how to feel about the character by indicating, you have created a performance *about* the character instead of presenting the character himself or herself. The audience may get the message but they won't feel involved. The essence of good acting, then, is to do what the character does, completely and precisely *as if for the first time and without adding anything superfluous.*

It is likely that you were guilty of some indicating when you were making believe in the previous exercise. You can learn to recognize indicating and avoid it by surrendering fully to your action. When you catch yourself *showing,* get back to *doing.* Repeat the previous exercise with this in mind.

EXERCISE 6.4   INDICATING

Repeat the Making Believe exercise (Exercise 6.3), but this time ask your audience members to signal by making some sort of noise whenever they feel that you are indicating. Compare their feedback with your own sense of being in action. Did you know when you were indicating? How strong is your impulse to *show* instead of *do,* or to do too much?

Automatic and Spontaneous Actions

As in real life, dramatic characters sometimes act without thinking; this is what Stanislavski called **automatic** action. In everyday life, we call this unconscious and automatic behavior *habit.*

When you are approaching a part, it is extremely useful to identify the habitual aspects of your character's behavior as soon as possible. You will want to strive to re-create the character's habits in yourself (only for purposes of playing the role, of course). Much of the behavior of characters may be habitual, things that they have been doing all their lives and that are "built into" them: their voice, walk, mannerisms, any special skills (like swordsmanship or knowing how to move in a hoop skirt). Through repeated rehearsal and homework, these habits should become as natural to you as they are to your character. This takes time, and there is no substitute for practice.

Besides these habits, there is another type of automatic action: Your character may experience important moments in which he or she is caught unawares by something and reacts *spontaneously*—as in moments of surprise or shock, or moments when the character suddenly understands or recognizes something astonishing. Such moments cannot be mechanically re-created and must happen afresh every time they are performed. In a sense, you have to forget what you are going to discover and then let yourself find it anew. This does not mean, however, that the form of the moment will vary wildly; you can learn to let it happen within parameters that serve the performance.

EXERCISE 6.5   **AUTOMATIC ACTIONS**

1. Review your scene with your partner. Does your character have any habitual traits? What do these things tell you about your character? What can you do to develop these habits in yourself for this role?
2. Are there moments of recognition, surprise, or impulse that must be spontaneous?

Defining Useful Objectives and Playable Actions

Baseball hitters rehearse their stance, grip, swing, and breathing. They study opposing pitchers. At the plate, they take note of the wind and the position of the fielders. As they begin to swing at a pitch, however, they cease to be aware of all these things and focus their total awareness on the ball. This single objective allows them to channel all their energy into their action, the swing. Having this single objective allows the batter to synthesize all his or her rehearsed and intuitive skills into a single complete action of mind and body that has tremendous power.

For you as an actor, the "ball" is your character's objective, what he or she is trying to accomplish at any given moment. Your focus on this single objective at the moment of action will overcome self-consciousness and give you power and control. Being focused on an objective propels you into action as you attempt to get what you want or need.

Since your energy must continually flow outward into the scene in order to keep the story moving, you want to define your actions in the most **playable** (i.e., *active*) way possible. First, you use a *simple verb phrase in transitive form*—that is, a verb that *involves* a *doing* directed *toward* someone else, such as "to flatter him." You avoid forms of the verb *to be* because this verb has no external object and its energy turns back on itself. You are never interested, for example, in "being angry" or "being a victim"; these states of being are not playable because their energy is directed inward. Strive instead for a *doing* in which your energy flows toward an external object.

Next, you select a verb that carries a sense of the particular **strategy** chosen by your character to achieve the objective. As in real life, your character will naturally select an action that seems to offer the greatest chance for success in the given circumstances and in relation to the other person(s) in the scene.

Experience has proven that objectives become more effective when they have three main qualities:

1. An objective needs to be *singular*; that is, you need to focus your energy on one thing rather than diffuse it by trying to do several things at once. Imagine a batter trying to hit two balls at the same time!
2. The most useful objective is in the *present*—something you want right now. Although your character's needs may be rooted in the past, his or her action at this moment is directed toward an objective in the immediate present.
3. An objective must be *personally important* to you. As you have already learned, personalizing an objective will energize you and empower your action.

It is easy to remember these three requirements by the acronym SIP: *singular, immediate,* and *personal.*

A useful example comes from a scene in *Death of a Salesman* in which Willy, an older traveling salesman who is having trouble staying awake while driving, goes to see his boss, Howard. Willy has an overall *scene objective* of wanting to persuade Howard to give him an assignment in town so he won't have to drive so much. When he enters the scene, he sees Howard playing with a new recorder, so Willy's *immediate objective* is to get Howard to stop playing with the recorder and to pay attention to him.

This objective is *singular* and *immediate.* It is also *personal* to Willy: If he can't get Howard's attention, he won't be able to ask for a job in town; if he doesn't get a job in town, he won't be able to be a successful salesman; if he can't be a successful salesman, he will think of himself as a failure in life. In this way, Willy's deepest, lifelong need for self-esteem lives in the present moment, and getting Howard's attention has all the urgency of a life-and-death struggle.

As an experienced salesman, Willy has learned to appeal to something the "client" would be interested in, so in this moment Willy chooses to flatter Howard by praising the recorder and the recording he has made of his family. The most complete description of Willy's action at this moment is expressed by the transitive verb phrase, *to flatter Howard by praising the recorder* in order to achieve the objective of *getting him to pay attention to me in a positive way.* This is SIP: singular, immediate, and deeply personal.

While you are learning to act, it may help you to form such a complete verbal description of your objectives and actions. Remember, however, that these verbal descriptions are valuable only insofar as they contribute to your actual experience of playing the scene. The ability to describe something comes from the analytical left side of the brain, whereas the creative work of performance originates in the intuitive right side of the brain. Although they can complement and augment one another wonderfully, the two sometimes get in each other's way.

EXERCISE 6.6   DEFINING OBJECTIVES AND ACTIONS

Working with your partner, read through your scene aloud several times. Then go through the scene together, and define each of your objectives and actions.

1. Make each objective SIP.
2. Describe each action with a transitive verb phrase that expresses the strategy being used.
3. Read through the scene in front of your class and feel the momentum that results when each of you has more specific and playable objectives and actions.

Obstacles and Counteractions

Since plays, films, and TV shows are about people interacting dramatically with one another, you must understand your objectives in ways that not only energize and focus on you by being SIP and transitive but also connect you with the other characters in the scene. The best way to achieve connectedness is to think of your objective as being *in* the other character, something specific you need from that person, *a change you want to bring about in the other character.*

In life, when we do something to try to make a change in someone else, we watch to see if what we are doing is working; if it is not, we try something else. This should be true on stage as well. Ask yourself, "How would I know I was achieving my objective? What changes might I see in the other character that would indicate that my approach is working?" In the Willy Loman scene, for instance, your first objective might be *to get Howard to look at me with interest.* Your full attention is on him, watching to see if your behavior is indeed producing the desired effect, or whether you might have to try a different approach (which in this case you eventually do).

In a well-crafted scene, the characters may be presenting *obstacles* to one another's actions and may even be acting *counter* to one another. Howard's insistence that Willy listen to the recording of his family, for example, is a *counteraction* to Willy's attempts to get Howard's attention. It is possible, in fact, that Howard begins to use the recording to avoid Willy.

As we do in real life, then, characters will select strategies that are designed to overcome obstacles, real or imagined, that stand between them and their objective. In Willy's case, the first obstacle is obvious: Howard isn't paying attention to him. On a deeper level, Willy may fear that Howard, with whom he has a strained relationship, will not be disposed to grant the favor Willy needs, and so Willy approaches Howard cautiously, eager to win his approval and fearful of antagonizing him. As you begin to work on a scene, then, it is useful to ask yourself not only "what is my objective here?" but also "what obstacle must I overcome to reach that objective?" Your strategic action will be chosen with that obstacle in mind.

EXERCISE 6.7 CONNECTING THE ACTION

1. Working with your partner, go through your scene and define each of your objectives as a change in the other character.
2. For each objective, identify the possible obstacle that must be overcome in order to achieve it.
3. Rehearse the scene with this awareness. Carry your scripts, but begin to move; don't worry about "blocking," and simply begin to allow your action to express itself in bodily movement within the space of the stage.
4. Discuss the scene with your partner or class. Did you achieve a stronger interaction? Did the action of the scene flow better?

Subtext

As do people in everyday life, a character will select an action that seems to offer the best chance for success in the given circumstances. Most often, this will be a direct action such as persuading, demanding, cajoling, or begging. However, sometimes there is an obstacle to direct action. An obstacle to direct action may be *internal*, like Willy's fear of angering Howard, or *external*, like Howard's obsession with the recorder. At such times, the character will try to get around the obstacle through an indirect approach, by saying or doing one thing when they really mean or want something else. In this case, although Willy *pretends* to be enjoying Howard's recording, he actually wants to get Howard to turn it off and pay attention. This kind of "hidden agenda" is called a *subtext*, because there is a difference between the surface activity, the text, and the hidden objective, the subtext. (Howard has his own subtext; he may be using the recorder to avoid a confrontation with Willy.)

How do you play a subtext? *You don't!* You will find that a good writer will always provide a surface activity through which the subtext may be expressed—in this case, Willy's pretended interest in the recorder. You must accept this surface activity as your immediate action: Do not attempt to bring the subtext to the surface by indicating it, by performing in a way that says "I'm only pretending to be interested; what I really want is his attention." Doing so will destroy the reality of the scene. For one thing, if the audience can see Willy's subtext, they will wonder why Howard can't. Trust that your simple awareness of subtext will be enough to properly color your actions.

EXERCISE 6.8 SUBTEXT

Again, rehearse your scene with your partner. Examine the objectives you defined in the previous exercise and see if any of them involve an *indirect* strategy. Does your character therefore have a subtext or hidden agenda? If so, why can't the action be expressed directly? What is the obstacle? Is it internal or external? Can you experience the subtext without bringing it to the surface of the scene?

Summary of Step 6

Drama shows us something happening as if before our eyes and for the first time. Thus, the good actor's performance is not *about* the character; it *is* the character living before our eyes as if for the first time. For this reason, we say that acting is doing, not showing or telling. Stanislavski based his system on the idea that everything an actor does in a performance has to be *justified* by connecting it to an internal need in the character. The main idea is that *need causes an action directed toward an objective.*

When you are totally focused on your dramatic task, you lose self-consciousness and undue awareness of the audience. Stanislavski called this *public solitude.* However, you never lose total awareness of the performance; rather you are able to operate on two levels simultaneously, the level of the character and his or her needs and world and the level of the actor making artistic choices. This essential ability is called *dual consciousness.* Some actors think they need to show the audience how the characters feel or what kind of people the characters are. When you *show* instead of *do*, you are *indicating*, and you lose the economy of a truthful performance. The audience may understand but won't believe or feel involved.

As in real life, dramatic characters sometimes act without thinking; this is what Stanislavski called **automatic** action. In everyday life, we call this unconscious and automatic behavior *habit*.

The best way to define a useful objective can be remembered by the acronym SIP: *singular, immediate,* and *personal.*

Since your energy must continually flow outward into the scene in order to keep the story moving, you want to define your actions in the most **playable** (i.e., *active*) way possible, using a *simple **verb** phrase in transitive form*—that is, a verb that *involves* a *doing* directed *toward* someone else, such as "to flatter him." You avoid forms of the verb *to be* because this verb has no external object; you are never interested, for example, in "being angry" or "being a victim."

Sometimes there is an obstacle to direct action. An obstacle to direct action may be *internal* or *external*. At such times, the character will, as people do in everyday life, try to get around the obstacle through an indirect approach, by saying or doing one thing when they really mean or want something else. This kind of "hidden agenda" is called a *subtext,* because there is a difference between the surface activity, the text, and the hidden objective, the subtext.

STEP 7

Beats, Scenes, Superobjective, and Spine

LEARNING OBJECTIVES

- Experience directly how individual actions and reactions flow together to produce scenes.
- Experiment with the ways in which scenes are shaped to produce satisfying dramatic experiences.
- Outline the concepts of Aristotle on the shape of drama with special emphasis on the idea of crisis, the turning point at which conflict is resolved.
- Explore how a scene may be broken down into units of action called "beats" and how beats connect to form the overall flow of a scene.
- Discover how beats relate directly to the objectives of your character, and how your character's objectives flow together to create a through-line driven by an overall life goal called the superobjective.

Now that you understand how a character's needs cause him or her to form objectives that in turn produce actions, you will next explore how those actions interact with those of other characters to produce a scene. Scenes happen because of a simple principle: Something happens to one character—they hear something or see something—that arouses them in some way, and they then say or do something in reaction. In turn, that character's action—his or her saying or doing—causes a reaction in some other character, and so on. Thus, the energy of the scene flows, being traded between the characters as they *act and react* to one another. Here is an exercise to help you experience that flow.

EXERCISE 7.1   IMPULSE CIRCLE

1. With your entire group, sit about eighteen inches apart in a large circle, in chairs or on the floor. Make the circle perfectly round. All group members put their left hands out palm up, and then rest their right hands lightly on top of the left hands of those to their right. The leader starts with a small, clean slap with his or her right hand. The slap is then passed on from person to person around the circle. Once the slap is moving well, try the following experiments:

   a. Focus your awareness on the slap as it moves around the circle. Begin to experience it as having a life of its own. Notice how it changes when you all do this.

   b. Now allow the slap to move as quickly as it can. See what happens when you "get out of its way." Do not force it to go faster; simply relax and react to it as instantaneously as possible.

   c. Now let the slap slow down. See how slow it can go without dying. Keep the external slap sharp and quick, but slow down the inner energy that produces the slap as it travels within each of you. Become aware of how the slap flows through both internal and external phases.

2. Drop your hands and discuss the many ways in which this exercise is like a scene in a performance. Consider these questions:

   a. What made it possible for the slap to flow around the group? How is this similar to the way a scene should flow in a performance?

   b. As you experienced the slap as having a life of its own, how did the nature of the flow change? Did your own experience of it change?

   c. Did allowing it to be the focus of your awareness reduce your self-consciousness?

   d. How much of the time was the slap "invisible" as a purely internal action? Could you experience the slap even when it was invisible?

   e. What was your relationship to the slap when it was passing through the others in the circle?

   f. What are some of the ways in which the slap can "die"? What are some of the ways in which we can fail to "pass it on"?

3. Repeat the exercise using a sound such as "ho" instead of a slap.

In this exercise, you experienced how a scene moves forward because energy passes between the characters. As you learned in the previous step, this action takes both external and internal forms; it is external when someone is saying or doing something, but much of the time—as you noticed in the exercise—it is internal as each participant receives the energy from others, reacts to it internally, and then passes it on through external action.

When energy is passed from one character to another, we call it an *interaction*. Each interaction is a connection in the flow of action and reaction that moves the scene and thereby the entire story forward. During rehearsals you will work to build each interaction in a scene, to make each of them real, and to make sure each moves toward the ultimate destination of the scene and the story as a whole.

You can experience this in a simple improvisation. Keep this exercise simple; it doesn't need to be long, complicated, witty, or dramatic. Just let it be as real and natural as possible. Go with whatever comes up, and see where it leads.

EXERCISE 7.2   **A SIMPLE ACTION SCENE**

With a partner, select a simple situation in which one of you wants to do something (e.g., to leave the room) while the other has a contradictory objective (e.g., to make him or her stay).

1. Without premeditation and with a minimum of words, both partners attempt to achieve their objectives in the most simple, direct terms.

2. Repeat the exercise, but this time each of you privately invent a powerful *need* for doing what you are doing. For example, one of you might imagine that if the other gets out, he or she will hurt someone you love; the other might imagine that he or she needs to get out to save a loved one. You needn't share or communicate what your needs are, nor do you and your partner need to agree on your needs.

3. Repeat the exercise again, this time imagining that you are both in a place where you cannot make much noise or movement, such as in a public library or at a funeral.

4. Discuss the experience of this exercise:
   a. Did you maintain your awareness of your objective throughout?
   b. Did you adjust what you did in reaction to what your partner did?
   c. What was the effect of adding strong needs?
   d. What was the effect of changing the circumstance?
   e. Did you notice how emotion and even a sense of character arose naturally from the action of the exercise?

The Shape of a Scene

The flow of action in the Impulse Circle, Exercise 7.1, was not necessarily dramatic. If a scene or play were to flow in this steady, repetitive way, it would soon become boring. In order to be dramatic or suspenseful, an event has to have a special kind of shape. You can experience this shape through this simple exercise.

EXERCISE 7.3   A DRAMATIC BREATH

1. Take a single, complete breath that is as *dramatic* as you can make it. Don't think about it; just do it!
2. Now consider the things you did to make the breath more dramatic. If you are in a group situation, discuss this and see if there was something that everyone did.

When trying this exercise for the first time, most people exaggerate their breath, making it louder; they may also add movement to the breath to make it more visible. Some people take a faster or slower breath than normal. These things alter the external aspects of the breath; they serve to make the breath more *theatrical*, not necessarily more *dramatic*. Do you understand the difference? Something can be theatrical without necessarily being dramatic; a sense of drama is deeper than external form; it implies an experience that involves us in a more fundamental way and can take many different external forms.

Consider those situations in real life that are naturally dramatic; we'll use a sporting event, a football, baseball, or basketball game, as an example. What are the conditions that make a game more dramatic? For one thing, games between teams that are evenly matched can be more dramatic because the sense of **conflict** is greater. *Conflict* literally means "to strike together," so any situation in which two strong forces are opposed creates a sense of drama. Most plays are driven by a central conflict between two opposing forces, usually embodied by a protagonist and an antagonist (in popular parlance, a hero and a villain). But conflict can exist even within a single person: The most famous example is Hamlet, who is torn between his need to avenge the murder of his father and his moral intelligence that tells him that revenge and murder are wrong, a conflict between his *will* and his *reason*. Another example is Tom in Tennessee Williams' *The Glass Menagerie*; he needs to leave home to find his own identity, but he feels an obligation to stay to support his sister and mother. This conflict between independence and responsibility is ***universal*** because all children feel something like it when it is time for them to leave the nest, even if their siblings and parents are not as needy as Laura and Amanda.

Besides a strong conflict, a game can be more dramatic if it is especially important or *significant*. Perhaps the championship is at stake, or the teams are long-standing rivals. In such significant situations, the *stakes are raised*, and the higher the stakes, the greater the drama can be. In the dramatic breath exercise, some of you may have increased the importance of your breath by taking a deeper breath; this deeper breath contained more energy and was therefore more significant than a normal breath. Notice, however, that a significant breath may not necessarily be bigger or louder; the significance of the breath depends not on these external qualities but on its inner *dynamic*, the amount of energy it contains. Imagine a situation in which you are hiding from a killer in a dark, silent room (like moments in the Guard and Thief game in Exercise 6.1); your life depends on making no noise or movement, and you are probably holding your breath, which is highly dramatic even though it is invisible and inaudible.

In addition to a strong conflict and high significance, the drama of a game depends on the *outcome being in doubt*. The closer the score of the game, the greater the drama can be; if one team gets too far ahead, we lose interest.

Think back to your dramatic breath: How might you put the outcome of your breath in doubt? The best way would be to hold it; while you are holding it, others might wonder, "When will he or she breathe out? How much longer can he or she hold it?" This is suspense in its purest form: *an aroused energy that wants to be released but is literally "held up."*

If the suspense of a game can last to the very last play, the drama is tremendous. In the same way, the longer you hold your breath, the more the suspense *builds* toward a climax. This is a common strategy in scenes and plays; the outcome is held in doubt as long as possible, thereby raising the level of suspense higher and higher. We call this rise and fall of energy the **arc** of the play or scene, and the greater the arc, the greater the drama. When you took your dramatic breath in the previous exercise, you may have increased the arc of your breath by building to a high point and then releasing it more deeply.

To sum up, then, our definition of a dramatic event is *a conflict of powerful forces in which the stakes are high and the outcome is in doubt so that suspense builds until a crisis is reached.* This applies equally to scenes and to entire plays.

Crisis

It was Aristotle who first described how the best kind of play is driven by an underlying conflict that is developed as the characters interact with one another, producing a flow of dramatic action that rises as suspense builds, until it reaches a **crisis** (which literally means "turning point,") at which point it reverses and falls toward a **climax** and resolution.

During the period of rising energy and growing suspense, we begin to wonder, "What will happen?" When the conflict is just on the verge of being resolved, suspense is at its peak. Everything that happens before the crisis leads toward it with *rising* energy, while everything after the crisis flows naturally from it with a *falling* sense of resolution. This, then, is the fundamental shape of Western drama (see Figure 7.1). It is a shape common to all of the performing arts—symphonies and ballets have it. It is the fundamental unit of rhythm, because it is the shape of a muscular contraction and relaxation. It is the fundamental shape of life itself, from birth to death. This is the shape of the breath you discovered in the previous exercise; a rising energy reaching a crisis, then releasing as a falling energy.

For example, in *The Glass Menagerie*, the idea of finding a gentleman caller who could marry Laura and thereby release Tom from his family obligations is established in the second scene of the play—this is the inciting incident as indicated in Figure 7.1. The main body of the play works out the details of the plan, and suspense mounts as Tom actually manages to bring Jim home. Suspense peaks as Jim dances with Laura and we sense that perhaps the plan might actually succeed; if it does, Jim will take over as the man of the house, and Tom will be released from his obligation without guilt. Sadly, however, the crisis reveals that the plan cannot work. Jim and Laura dance and kiss, but a moment later, Jim reveals that he is engaged to another girl. The climax flows quickly from this crisis; Laura falls back even more deeply into her dependency,

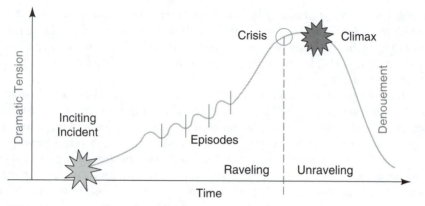

FIGURE 7.1

The Most Common Shape of a Play in Western Drama

Amanda blames Tom for the failure of the plan, and Tom finally storms out for good, wracked by guilt.

The shape of energy rising toward a crisis can be seen not only in the play as a whole, but also in the shape of the scenes within the play. Unlike an entire play, however, a single scene does not have a complete resolution because the scene must lead us on to the scenes that follow. Typically, then, a scene will end by raising a further question that will propel us into the following scenes. We ask, "Now that this has happened, what will happen next?" For example, in the scene between Willy and Howard in *Death of a Salesman*, the crisis of the scene occurs when Howard fires Willy, and immediately, we begin to wonder, "What will Willy do now that he has lost his job?"

The best way to identify the crisis of a scene or a play is to work backward from the end, looking for the moment at which the outcome hangs most in the balance. Ask yourself: "Given the way it comes out, what is the last moment at which the play or scene might have turned out differently?" In the scene from *Death of a Salesman*, it is the moment when Willy yells at Howard, causing Howard to fire him; in *The Glass Menagerie*, it is the moment after the kiss, when Jim reveals that he is engaged to another and cannot go on seeing Laura. This strategy of "reading backward" is a valuable tool for analyzing both scenes and plays.

EXERCISE 7.4   THE SHAPE OF YOUR SCENE

Working with your scene partner, discuss your scene. Think backward from the end:

1. What is the main thing that happens in this scene? In other words, what is the "big question" in this scene?
2. What makes this question significant? What is at stake?
3. What is the source of suspense? How is the outcome kept in doubt?
4. Where is the crisis, when the question is on the verge of being answered?

Units of Action, or Beats

Plays are usually divided into acts, acts into scenes, and scenes themselves may be divided into smaller units of action called *beats*. The word *beat* may come from *bit*, meaning "a small part." Stanislavski used the term "unit of action" for what we commonly call a beat today. In any case, a beat has its own dramatic shape, with an underlying conflict and a rising action leading to a crisis. Beats, like scenes, do not have much resolution since they must lead us on into the next beat in order to continue the flow of the scene.

For example, consider the beginning of the scene in *Death of a Salesman* when Willy enters and sees Howard playing with a new recorder. As we have said, Willy's objective in this scene is to get an assignment in town so he will not have to continue driving; when he sees Howard with the recorder, his immediate objective is to get Howard to stop playing with the recorder and to pay attention to him. Ever the good salesman, Willy flatters Howard by feigning interest in the recorder, and finally Howard looks up and says, "Say, aren't you supposed to be in Boston?" This is the turning point that ends the first beat of the scene; it is called a **beat change**.

This first beat of the scene has its own underlying conflict (Willy trying to get Howard's attention, Howard trying to ignore Willy) and a crisis (Howard finally paying attention to Willy). This beat is unified by the fact that each character has one immediate objective throughout (Willy to get Howard's attention, Howard to ignore Willy). A beat change occurs when one of the characters changes his or her objective, or changes the strategic action he or she is pursuing to reach an objective even if the objective itself does not change.

For example, Willy persists in his objective of getting a spot in town, but Howard's resistance forces him to try several strategies, such as flattering, persuading, and demanding. Each of these changes in strategies by Willy leads us into a new beat, and each beat change can be felt as a change in the flow of the scene as it turns a corner and moves in a new direction. Because this change is felt as a pulse in the rhythm of the scene, the term "beat" is a good description of the musical shape of a scene.

You can begin to see how every small unit of action is part of a larger pattern and derives its meaning and function from the way it fits into and contributes to that larger pattern. The individual interactions between characters work together to form the units of action we call beats; the beats work together to form scenes; and the scenes flow together to lead us to the main crisis and climax of the entire story.

This idea may be more easily understood by the muscles than the mind, so let's try a physical exercise to experience it.

EXERCISE 7.5   **UNITS OF ACTION**

Perform each of the following actions, and experience the dramatic potential of each. Remember to focus on the crisis in each pattern: Treat all that goes before as leading up to the crisis and all that follows as flowing from it.

1. Experience the dramatic shape of a single step. Find the crisis of one step, and tie your breathing to the shape of the step.
2. Experiment with differently shaped steps: a long rise, a long crisis, and a quick release; then a short rise, a short crisis, and a long release; and so on.
3. Take three steps experienced as one phrase, with the crisis in the third step. The first two steps have mini-crises of their own, but they also lead up to the main crisis of the unit in the third step. Let your breath parallel the pattern of your steps.
4. Now try nine steps, divided into three units of three steps each, with the crisis of this larger pattern in the last group (as in Figure 7.2). Try it again with the crisis in the first group of steps.
5. Invent patterns of your own; add sound.

In this exercise you experienced small units of action (individual steps) forming a larger pattern of action that has a dramatic shape of its own. Likewise, these larger phrases can be connected into still larger patterns, which again have shapes of their own. On all these levels, the fundamental shape of rise, crisis, and release is the same, even though the proportion of the parts may be different.

Once you have understood the structure of the scene and the way it serves the entire play, your attention as an actor is free to be on the immediate moment, the here and now. You are in the moment, but are also aware of how this moment contributes to the beat of which it is a part, how this beat contributes to the scene of which it is a part, and ultimately how the scene contributes to the overall structure of the play. This is an important and fundamental concept that will be of great importance to you as an actor.

To develop a deeper understanding of the importance of scene structure, let's take an example from a scene in *A Raisin in the Sun*. We begin with the given circumstances: It is morning on a work day in the tiny, crowded kitchen of the Lee apartment; as usual, Ruth is fixing breakfast for her husband, Walter. The night before, Walter's friend Willy suggested a scheme to open a liquor store.

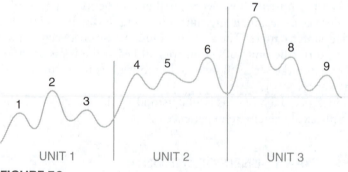

FIGURE 7.2

Units of Action

Here, nine steps are divided into three units (beats) that go together to produce one larger pattern (a scene). Each step has a crisis, as does each beat, and the overall crisis of the scene is in step 7.

Willy's idea was that Walter, Willy, and another friend (Bobo) would each invest $10,000 to open the store. It is no coincidence that Walter's father has recently died, leaving a $10,000 life insurance payment; as we will learn later, Willy knows this and has concocted the whole scheme in order to cheat Walter out of his insurance money. But for now, Walter thinks the scheme is legitimate, and he comes in to breakfast, having decided that he wants to invest the insurance money in Willy's scheme. Walter knows that he must first overcome the objections of his devout mother, Mama, who wants nothing to do with a liquor store and who has other plans for the money. Walter has decided to persuade his wife Ruth to approach Mama on his behalf.

Looking at the play as a whole, we see that Walter has a deep overall need to win respect and self-esteem. (We call this his *superobjective*.) He has chosen the objective of starting a liquor store hoping it will satisfy that need. In this particular scene, that larger objective requires that he persuade Ruth to intercede with Mama. (This is his *scene objective*.) Ruth, however, resists. Walter tries several strategies to win her over, each of which is a separate beat: He tries *to make her feel guilty* by reminding her that he missed a similar opportunity once before; he tries *to shame her* into "supporting her man"; and finally he *pleads* with her to save him from his despair. Each of these specific actions is driven by his need to win her over, and that need, in turn, is driven by his deep need to win self-esteem. Walter's *beat objectives* are strategies driven by his *scene objective*, which, in turn, is driven by his *superobjective*.

Ruth, for her part, is driven by the need to deal with her secret pregnancy, which at this point she plans to terminate. She mistrusts Walter's friends (with good reason) and dislikes the shady aspects of Willy's scheme, which involves bribing city officials. What she most emphatically does *not* need at this moment is to be drawn into one of Walter's harebrained schemes. Thus, her needs are in direct conflict with Walter's needs and she finally explodes as she tells him, "Then go to work," which has the subtextual meanings of "Stop your whining," "Do the right thing," and "Leave me alone!" Her outburst is the crisis of the scene and each preceding beat builds up to that crisis.

As you become more experienced with this way of working, you will sometimes be able to recognize beat changes early in your preparation; this early analysis of the structure of a scene is called a **breakdown**, or **scenario**. The technique of breaking a scene down will help you to feel the rhythm and shape of your scene as it was structured by the playwright.

EXERCISE 7.6   BREAKING DOWN YOUR SCENE

1. Working with your partner, come to a mutual agreement about where the overall crisis of your scene occurs.
2. Make a rough breakdown of the scene by identifying the units of action within it.
3. Define your character's action and objective in each beat. Remember to express each action as a transitive verb that is SIP, and think of each objective as a desired change in the other character.

4. Rehearse the scene together to emphasize and clarify its rhythms and the beat changes. Move so as to physicalize the beat changes by shifting your positions in relation to one another, but at this stage in the scene's development do not worry about blocking; move according to your impulses.

5. Carrying your script in hand if necessary, perform the scene in front of your group; ask the group members to note where they feel the beats changing and where they feel the crisis of the entire scene to be. Afterward, compare their responses to your breakdown.

Making Connections

Now that you are well into the rehearsal of your scene, you and your partner are beginning to shape and specify the sequence of actions and reactions that form the flow that binds the scene together. As you feel the connectedness of every moment with every other moment, your *through-line* begins to emerge, and the scene begins "to play," to flow under its own power. You no longer have to *make* things happen; you can *let* them happen. As a result, your scene begins to feel simpler and shorter.

> EXERCISE 7.7   **MAKING CONNECTIONS**
>
> Work through your scene with your partner, allowing either of you to stop the rehearsal at any point when you do not feel connected to the flow of the action, and when your partner is not "making" you do what you must do next.
>
> At each point of difficulty, examine the moments that led up to it; what does either of you need from the other to induce the next action? Work together so that every moment of the scene grows organically out of the flow of action and reaction, so that each of you causes your partner to do whatever he or she does next.
>
> *Note:* Do not tell your partner what to do; instead, ask for what you *need*, and leave it to your partner to provide it. You might, for example, say something like "I need to be more threatened by that," but leave it to your partner to determine how best to threaten you.

This exercise will help you to realize that a difficulty at one point in a scene is often caused by problems earlier in the scene, or even earlier in the play. Don't always try to fix a problem by making an immediate adjustment; trace back and see if you can clear it up by adjusting some earlier action, value, or relationship.

The Through-Line and the Superobjective

You now understand that dramatic action is structured on several levels: *Interactions* work together to make up units of action called *beats*, beats work together to make up *scenes*, and scenes form the overall shape of the entire play.

These levels of action relate directly to the inner life of your character because you have an objective on each level: In each interaction you are striving toward your character's *beat objective*, each of these beat objectives stem from your character's *scene objective*, and all these scene objectives can be seen as springing from a deep, overall objective that is your character's *superobjective*.

The idea of a superobjective is easier to grasp if you think of it as a life goal or a guiding principle governing your character's behavior, often on an unconscious level. Such drives are basic, like the desire for love, respect, security, or aliveness. They can also be "negatives," such as the avoidance of failure or ridicule. And they can be idealistic, such as a passion for justice or freedom. In real life people often have life goals that influence their behavior, but it is not easy to identify someone's superobjective unless you have a lot of experience with the person and know him or her well. In a similar way, your understanding of your character's superobjective will develop gradually as you rehearse; it will be the *result* of your experience of the role, not a prerequisite for it. Nonetheless, it may be useful to form a general idea of the superobjective early on, knowing that your understanding may change as your work progresses.

For example, consider the scene from *Death of a Salesman* in which Willy, hoping to get a new assignment that will not require driving, finds Howard engrossed in his new recorder. Willy's immediate objective is to get Howard's attention so he can move toward his larger objective of getting an assignment in town. This objective is connected directly to Willy's superobjective, to be a successful salesman, which for Willy is a way *to prove himself a worthy human being by earning money and respect.* (Notice that you define the superobjective in the same way as any other objective, by using a transitive verb.) You might even find a line from the play that sums it up; for example, Willy says, "Be liked and you will never want."

If we follow each of Willy's immediate objectives throughout the play, we see in each case how he is led from objective to objective in pursuit of his superobjective. The logic of this sequence of objectives striving toward the superobjective is called the **through-line** of the role. Stanislavski described it like this:

> In a play the whole stream of individual minor objectives, all the imaginative
> thoughts, feelings and actions of an actor should converge to carry out
> this superobjective....Also this impetus toward the superobjective must be
> continuous throughout the whole play.[1]

Stanislavski once said that each of a character's actions fits into the through-line like vertebrae in a spine. Therefore, some actors call the through-line the **spine** of the role.

Identifying your character's through-line of action as being driven by his or her superobjective can help you to better understand each of your specific objectives, connecting each to the character's deepest needs and desires. It can also help you to see that the sequence of objectives has a single driving force; thus,

---

[1]Constantin Stanislavski, *An Actor's Handbook*, trans. and ed. Elizabeth Reynolds Hapgood (New York: Theatre Arts Books, 1936), p. 56. Copyright © 1936, 1961, 1963 by Elizabeth Reynolds Hapgood.

you can play through each moment and achieve both unity and momentum (good **pace**) in your performance.

Your character's superobjective may be conscious or (more commonly) unconscious. If the character is not conscious of it, you—the actor—will have to take it fully into account as you work, but you should not let your knowledge of it as an actor "contaminate" your character's reality. Remember the idea of dual consciousness: What you know as an actor is not the same as what your character knows, and you should not allow your actor awareness to contaminate your character's mind. The acting teacher Lee Strasberg once said that the hardest thing about acting is "not knowing what you know."

Whether or not your character is conscious of his or her superobjective, it functions as an underlying principle that affects all of their actions and establishes their attitude toward life. Willy Loman, for example, tries to earn self-esteem through selling; he confuses success as a salesman with success as a human being. Eventually, he is no longer able to sell either his products or himself, and his last "sale" becomes his suicide, making the insurance money the family will collect his last "paycheck." Thus, this final, desperate act (which is the climax of the play) is the fulfillment of Willy's tragically misguided way of pursuing his superobjective.

By experiencing how each moment, beat, and scene of your character's behavior is driven by his or her superobjective, you will fulfill what Stanislavski called the actor's main task: *to understand how every moment of the performance contributes to the reason why the play was written.*

EXERCISE 7.8   IDENTIFYING THE SUPEROBJECTIVE

1. Taking the entire play into account, describe your character's superobjective, using a transitive verb phrase such as "to be thought of as a worthy human being."
2. Specify the kind of strategies your character commonly uses to try to achieve this superobjective, such as "to be thought of as a worthy human being by making sales and earning the smiles of my clients, friends, and even my family."
3. Is your character conscious or unconscious of this life goal? Is there a line from the play that sums it up?

Summary of Step 7

Action is structured on several levels: *Interactions* work together to make up units of action called *beats*, beats work together to make up *scenes*, and scenes form the overall shape of the entire play. These levels of action relate directly to the inner life of your character because you have an objective on each level: In the immediate moment you will be striving toward your character's *beat objective*, each of these beat objectives stem from your character's *scene objective*, and all these scene objectives can be seen as springing from a deep, overall objective that is your character's *superobjective*. The logic of this sequence of objectives striving toward the superobjective is called the *through-line* of the role, or sometimes called the spine.

Scenes are a flow of dramatic action driven by a conflict and moving toward a resolution. The energy of the scene flows, being traded between the characters as they *act and react* to one another. When energy is passed from one character to another, we call it an *interaction*. Each interaction is a connection in the flow of action and reaction that moves the scene and thereby the entire story.

A dramatic event is *a conflict of powerful forces in which the stakes are high and the outcome is in doubt, building to a crisis, which is followed by a climax*. This applies equally to scenes and to entire plays. As the characters interact with one another, their interaction produces a flow of dramatic action that rises as *suspense* builds, until it reaches a *crisis* (which literally means "turning point,") at which point it reverses and falls toward a climax and resolution.

Plays are usually divided into acts, acts into scenes, and scenes themselves may be divided into smaller units of action called *beats*. Stanislavski used the term "unit of action" for what we commonly call a beat today.

When one of the characters changes his or her objective, the change leads us into a new beat. This beat change can be felt as a change in the flow of the action of the scene as it turns a corner and moves in a new direction. Because this turn is felt as a pulse in the rhythm of the scene, the term "beat" is a good description of the musical shape of the flow of a scene's rhythm.

Your attention as an actor is on the immediate moment, the here and now, but you are also aware of how this moment contributes to the beat of which it is a part, how each beat contributes to the scene of which it is a part, and ultimately how each scene contributes to the overall structure of the play as a whole. You will sometimes be able to recognize beat changes as you read a scene; this early analysis of the structure of a scene is called a breakdown, or scenario. The technique of breaking a scene down will help you to feel the rhythm and shape of your scene as it was structured by the playwright.

As you feel the connectedness of every moment with every other moment, your through-line begins to emerge, and the scene begins "to play," to flow under its own power. You no longer have to *make* things happen; you can *let* them happen. As a result, your scene begins to feel simpler and shorter.

Your character's objectives in each beat and scene can be seen as springing from an overall superobjective, a life goal or a guiding principle governing your character's behavior, often on an unconscious level. The logic of this sequence of objectives striving toward the superobjective is called the through-line of the role. Stanislavski once said that each of a character's actions fits into the through-line like vertebrae in a spine so some actors call the through-line the spine of the role.

STEP 8

The Foundations
of Character

LEARNING OBJECTIVES

- Identify the qualities provided by the writer to create a believable characterization that functions effectively within the overall scheme of the story.
- Explore the traits in four categories: physical (age, gender, physique), social (general and specific relationships), psychological (specific mental processes), and moral (values, beliefs, ethics).
- Consider how these traits function within the particular world of the story.
- Discover how character is expressed mainly in relationship with others, so that in a real sense all the actors in a play are responsible for creating all the characters, not just their own.

The character you create as an actor is not something that you can entirely predetermine by analysis or imagination; rather, it emerges gradually from the process of exploration and discovery in the give-and-take of rehearsal with your fellow actors. Your character must grow in relationship to the way the other characters in the play are being developed by the other actors, and it is your living experience of your character's action in relation to the other characters that truly generates that version of yourself which will become the eventual characterization.

This is how character develops in real life, where we call character "personality." Think about how your own personality has developed over the years and how often you "create a character" in real life. In various circumstances and relationships, you pursue your needs by behaving in certain ways, doing and saying certain things in certain ways to other people, and reacting to the things they do and say to you. It is this interaction with your world that shapes and expresses your character in everyday life. It is an ongoing process: As your circumstances, needs, and relationships change, they cause changes in you as a person.

You play a role every time you enter a social situation. In fact, you play several roles every day—student, son or daughter, friend, employee; each role has its own appropriate behavior, speech, thought, and feelings—your own little cast of characters! This fact was noticed many years ago by the psychologist William James, who said that our personalities are actually composed of many social roles. He called these roles our various *me's*. Behind the me's, of course, is one consciousness, which he called our *I*. But our I is not rigid and is expressed through all of our me's, even though some of them may be quite different from one another.

We may even experience situations in which two or more of our me's come into conflict with one another. If you are busy being "buddy" with your friends, the arrival of a parent may cause an uncomfortable conflict between your role as buddy and your role as a son or daughter. Such situations are inherently dramatic and often occur in plays, as when Hamlet is torn between the roles of son to Gertrude, lover to Ophelia, friend to Rosencrantz and Guildenstern, and avenger to Claudius.

As you think about how you play various roles in your life, you will also notice that your sense of "I" tends to flow into whichever "me" you are being at the moment. Some of your me's may be more—or less—comfortable than others, but they are all versions of you. If you are in a circumstance that forces you to behave in a certain way and you allow yourself to remain in that situation for a time, you start to become the person appropriate to that situation; you develop a new me, which in turn becomes part of your I.

In the same way, when you work as an actor, you will learn to let your I flow into the new me of each role you play, even when that me is quite different from your everyday self. The qualities of each new me have been determined by the writer, who has also created a new set of circumstances, a new world, in which the new me lives. One of your most important skills as an actor will be *to allow your I to flow fully and freely into the new me of the role and its world.* You do this not to "be yourself" on stage but to develop a new *version* of yourself, perhaps one that is quite different from your everyday self, but one that is nevertheless "natural" to you, truthful to the character and the character's world as created by the writer, and appropriate to the artistic purpose for which the role was created.

Stanislavski called this process the **Magic If**, which works as follows: As you consider the role you are about to play, ask yourself, "*If* I were in the circumstances of the character, and *if* I wanted what the character wants, and *if* I allowed myself to do the things the character does to try to satisfy those needs, who would I become?"

The answer will be found in actual experience. As you rehearse and begin to experience yourself living in the character's world, wanting what he or she wants (or things important to you that are *analogous* to the character's needs) and saying and doing what he or she says and does to try to satisfy those needs, you will naturally, "magically," start to develop a new me that will modify your thoughts, feelings, behavior, and even your body and voice toward that new version of yourself that will be your special way of playing the role. This is true *transformation.*

This ability to become a fictitious character, to completely believe in the Magic If and actively enter a make-believe world and character, is something we all had naturally as children. And it is this childlike capacity for make-believe that we need to rediscover as actors, however much we empower it through our adult sense of purpose and technique.

EXERCISE 8.1   CHARACTER IN LIFE

For the next few days, observe your own behavior toward those around you. Notice the ways you present yourself differently in various circumstances.

1. Notice changes in your physical behavior.
2. Notice changes in your voice, manner of speaking, and choice of words.
3. Notice your choice of clothing and the "props" you use.
4. Notice changes in the way you think and feel.
5. Most of all, notice how you naturally tend to "become" each of the roles you are playing.

Having begun to understand how personality evolves in real life, you are ready to apply this same understanding to your work on your scene.

EXERCISE 8.2   CHARACTER IN YOUR SCENE

With your partner, begin to rehearse your scene with an awareness of the influence of the Magic If:

1. Review the givens of your scene and allow yourself to enter into them as fully as you can.
2. Review your understanding of your character's wants and needs; allow yourself to have, in your own way, those same wants and needs, *or ones that are analogous to them* that are important to you in your life.
3. As you rehearse your scene, experience your character's objectives and actions as if they were your own.
4. Notice how the repeated experience of the scene begins to change the way you think and feel. Notice changes in your voice or body, but don't try to generate these changes artificially. Simply notice how you naturally tend to "become" the person who lives in this world, wants what they want, and does what they do to try to achieve those objectives in relation to the other characters.

To sum up and emphasize this central concept: When an actor creates a character, he or she uses a process that is similar to how personality is formed and evolves in everyday life. In everyday life, we interact with our world and the people in it and the cumulative effect of those experiences and circumstances shapes who we are; as our relationships or circumstances change, we change with them. Rehearsals are an intensified and focused version of this real-life process through the operation of the Magic If. You imaginatively enter into the character's circumstances, experience his or her needs as if they were your own, form objectives aimed at satisfying those needs, and allow yourself to do and say what the character does (his or her actions) to pursue those objectives. The power of these experiences shapes a new version of you, a new "me" for your "I," and so the dramatic character evolves in the same way that our personality evolves in real life. As social psychologist Erving Goffman puts it: "…life itself is a dramatically enacted thing.…In short, we all act better than we know how."[1]

Of course, these everyday abilities must be heightened, purified, and brought within the control of a purposeful discipline. As acting teacher and psychologist Brian Bates says: "…the actor must develop depths of self-knowledge and powers of expression far beyond those with which most of us are familiar."[2] You are now launched on the path of developing your everyday acting skills into the greater power of artistic technique. Up to this point, you have begun to prepare the physical, vocal, and mental skills you will need as an actor. In the remaining steps in this book, you will begin to apply yourself to the preparation of a stage performance, through which you will explore techniques and concepts that will help you to recognize, focus, and strengthen the natural actor you already are.

Character Traits

As we said in Step 1, your character was created to do a specific job within the scheme of the play as a whole. We called this the *dramatic function* of the character, and understanding this function will inspire and guide your work in rehearsal. Too often actors approach their characters so personally that they begin to forget the larger purpose for which their characters were created. Without a larger sense of purpose, you might create a character who is alive and believable, but who doesn't do the intended job within the story as a whole. The audience might be impressed by such a performance, but the story would suffer and you would have failed in your main responsibility. According to Stanislavski, the actor's most important task is *to understand how every moment of the performance and every aspect of characterization contributes to the reason why the play was written.*

"The reason why the play was written" encompasses not only the story being told but the particular meaning that story is meant to impart. The writer has given each character certain traits so that he or she can believably perform the actions necessary to fulfill his or her contribution to the story and also to endow those actions with the meaning the story requires.

Your work on your character should begin with an examination of the traits of your character as established by the writer, for these are the parameters within which you work as you begin to find your own, personal way of manifesting those traits in a living performance.

---

[1] Erving Goffman, *The Presentation of Self in Everyday Life* (New York: Doubleday, 1959), pp. 71–74. Copyright © by Erving Goffman.

[2] Brian Bates, *The Way of the Actor* (Boston: Shambhala, 1987), p. 7.

Function Traits

Characters are given certain traits that make their actions seem "natural." Aristotle called these the *function traits* because they permit characters to believably fulfill their dramatic functions within a story. In *Death of a Salesman*, for example, Willy Loman is a man who, like many of his generation, measures his value as a human being by his success in his work. He is a man who sells; eventually we realize that he is selling himself. He feels that he is worthless until he persuades others, even his own sons, of his value, and he does this not only by making money but also by earning the smiles and respect of his clients. When he can no longer succeed as a salesman, his self-esteem is so damaged that he finally makes the only "sale" he has left as his suicide enables his family to collect on his life insurance.

Arthur Miller has endowed this story with a particular meaning, which makes it a commentary on the destructiveness of the overly materialistic values of American society. We can say, then, that Willy's dramatic function is to represent the many people who are encouraged by our highly materialistic and competitive society to think that earning money and approval is the only source of self-esteem. Such people, like Willy, confuse material and spiritual values, and this, Miller is saying, can be a tragic consequence of the American Dream. Sadly, in our age of corporate downsizing and outsourcing, and at a time when entire professions are being made obsolete by technology, we see many people in Willy Loman's situation, and the play is becoming more and more relative and poignant for us.

A Raisin in the Sun by Lorraine Hansberry is also a play about the American Dream. The title of the play refers to a poem by Langston Hughes in which unfulfilled dreams shrivel up "like a raisin in the sun." Every member of the Younger family has a dream: Walter, like Willy Loman, wants to win self-esteem by making money. As he tells his wife, "I got to take hold of this here world, baby!" His scheme to open a liquor store is driven by his sense of failure: All he has to give his sons "is stories about how rich white people live...." He is so driven that, like Willy Loman, he makes misguided choices. By the end of the play, however, it is Mama's dream of a home of their own that prevails because it will unite the family; they will risk fighting racial discrimination because they believe they can succeed if they stick together. Each member of the Younger family has a central function trait: Walter is desperate to feel like a worthy father, Beneatha wants to find and fulfill her own identity by serving the world meaningfully, and Mama wants to bind her family together.

In Tennessee Williams's *The Glass Menagerie*, Tom longs for the freedom to pursue his own life and thereby to discover his own identity. He is held back by his sense of obligation to his family, especially to his disabled sister. He is "the man of the house" and fears that if he leaves, it will be very hard for Laura and Amanda to get by. His only hope, then, is to find a replacement "man of the house" for Laura. Jim the gentleman caller is that hope, and it is a bitter irony that Jim fails to fulfill that hope because he is himself consumed by another example of the American Dream gone wrong. As he tells Laura:

> *Knowledge*—Zzzzzp! *Money*—Zzzzzzp!—*Power*! That's the cycle democracy is built on!

In each of these cases, the playwright has provided central function traits that drive the characters to behave in ways that serve their stories—Willy Loman's insecurity, Walter Younger's ambition to "beat the system," and Tom Wingfield's need to escape his obligations in search of his own identity, all are the main motivating forces that make the events of the plays seem natural and even inevitable.

Recognition Traits

At a deep level, all of the characters we have mentioned are driven by fundamental human needs like the desire for self-esteem, love, or security. Drama, after all, portrays universal patterns of human experience that we can all recognize and share, and function traits are usually universal in this way. There is another kind of trait, however, that well-drawn characters must possess. According to Aristotle in *The Poetics*, we must be able to *recognize* characters as fellow human beings, even if we do not like them. A performance must therefore include traits that round out the character and make us recognize him or her as a real and specific human being who is in some way like us or like people we know or know about. We call these *recognition traits*, which are usually more specific to an individual character and less universal than function traits.

Arthur Miller tells us, for example, that Willy's wife loves him in spite of "his mercurial nature, his temper, his massive dreams and little cruelties." Miller also shows us that Willy tries hard to be fun with his male friends and is a bit of a flirt with the women. His mercurial nature makes him quick to anger but just as quick to be remorseful and apologetic. His great pride may sometimes drive him to be cruelly demeaning to others, as in his contempt for Charley's son Bernard. All these traits help to round out Willy as a recognizable human being.

Although some recognition traits are provided by the writer, this is an area in which the actor may contribute personal touches to a role that make it his or her own unique creation. For example, Willy might be a bit of a dandy in the way he dresses and carries himself in scenes from his earlier life, but he might be so disheartened later in life that he has let himself go in both body and dress. When Dustin Hoffman played him, Willy had even developed a quivering hand and lip. There are many such recognition traits an actor might give Willy, some of which might be surprising—people, after all, are complex. But whatever traits the actor may contribute out of his own personality and imagination must never be allowed to obscure Willy's main function trait of profound insecurity.

We can classify all traits of character in four categories, as outlined here by theater historian Oscar Brockett:

> The first level of characterization is physical and is concerned only with such basic facts as sex, age, size, and color. Sometimes a dramatist does not supply all of this information, but it is present whenever the play is produced, since actors necessarily give concrete form to the characters...
>
> The second level is social. It includes a character's economic status, profession or trade, religion, family relationships—all those factors that place him in his environment.

The third level is psychological. It reveals a character's habitual responses, attitudes, desires, motivations, likes and dislikes—the inner workings of the mind, both emotional and intellectual, which precede action... the psychological is the most essential level of characterization.

The fourth level is moral. Although implied in all plays, it is not always emphasized. It is most apt to be used in serious plays, especially tragedies.[3]

As you prepare to rehearse, you should learn all you can about the character from the evidence within the text itself. To summarize Brockett's categories, the basic traits to look for are these:

1. *Physical traits* such as the character's age, body type, and any special physical traits or skills
2. *Social traits* such as his or her culture and historical period, social and economic class, educational background, and family background
3. *Psychological traits* such as intelligence, quickness, sensitivities, obsessions, or phobias
4. *Moral traits* such as beliefs and values, including religious and political views

Of these, the last two are of particular interest in most modern plays. For the psychological traits, consider the mental processes of your character. Are they:

1. Simple or complex?
2. Fast or slow?
3. Rigid or flexible?
4. Precise or vague?
5. Rational or intuitive?
6. Global or sequential?

The moral level of character refers to your character's values. Most important are the following:

1. Their sense of right and wrong
2. Their sense of beauty
3. Their religious beliefs
4. Their political convictions

Look not only at character descriptions provided by the writer but also at traits implied by the character's action and background. Consider also things said about the character by other characters (remembering that their views may be biased). If there isn't much information supplied by the writer, it may be useful for you to invent some for yourself, although you must be careful to do this in a manner that supports and extends the character's function within the play.

---

[3]Oscar G. Brockett, The Theatre: An Introduction, 3rd ed. (New York: Holt, Rinehart & Winston, 1974), pp. 39–40.

EXERCISE 8.3   **INVENTORY OF CHARACTER TRAITS**

Examine the evidence in the script about your character's traits. Make a list that summarizes his or her physical, social, psychological, and moral traits.

Remember that all this basic information about the character's traits is intended only to inspire and guide your exploration in rehearsal; you must not simply "put it on" as if it were a mask or costume. You will have to discover the inner world of the character that brings these traits to life—that is, the inner qualities that lie behind the external appearances—and in the process you will begin to find that new version of yourself that will be your special way of playing the role. This is what Stanislavski meant by the process of *transformation*. It will be the greatest creative and personal contribution you will make to your performance and the foundation of all the other work you will do on the role.

Summary of Step 8

As in everyday life, character develops out of a person's interactions with his or her world and especially relationships with other people. According to William James, our personalities in everyday life are composed of many social roles he called our me's; behind the me's there is one consciousness, our I. As an actor you will learn to let your I flow into the new me of each role you play so that it becomes "natural" to you, truthful to the character, and appropriate to the artistic purpose for which the role was created.

Stanislavski called this process the Magic If. If you live in the world of the character, and if you need what the character needs, and if you do the things the character does to satisfy those needs, you will naturally start to modify your thoughts, feelings, behavior, and even your body and voice; a new me begins to form—that new version of yourself that will be your special way of playing the role.

What an actor does, then, is similar to what you do every day in real life. In this sense, you are already an actor, and you already have many of the skills you will need to perform. It is the development of these everyday acting skills into the greater power of artistic technique that is the aim of your study.

A writer creates a character to believably perform the actions necessary to fulfill his or her dramatic function and gives the character certain traits that are consistent with those actions. Aristotle called these *function* traits because they permit characters to believably fulfill their dramatic functions within a story. A performance must also include traits that round out the character and make us recognize him or her as a real and specific human being, and we call these *recognition* traits, and this is an area in which an actor may contribute personal touches to a role that make it his or her own unique creation. Character traits can be of four main types: physical (age, body type, etc.), social (relationships with other characters), psychological (qualities of mind), and moral (beliefs and values).

STEP 9

Personalization

LEARNING OBJECTIVES

- Explore the various ways in which you can internalize the character, using yourself to best advantage as you search for your own way of playing the role.
- Find how you can feel the needs of the character for yourself, enter the workings of the character's mind, and live through the choices the character makes.
- Use experiential exercises such as the creation of an inner monologue, autobiography, and diary for your personal entry into the life of the character.

Every role, Stanislavski said, is a marriage between actor and character. No two actors will play a role the same way; each will contribute unique qualities that come from the actor's self and way of seeing the role. What is important is that the actor reaches out to inhabit the character in a way that serves the needs of the play, and does not merely suck the character into himself or herself, using it as a vehicle for mere self-expression without regard for the ideas and form of the play.

Another way of saying this, as we have stressed before, is that every character you create will be a new version of yourself—a new "me" of your "I"—which is found by letting yourself reach out to inhabit the world, qualities, and thoughts of the character. You possess a vast personal potential. If you can engage your own energy in your character's actions within the scripted world and can make that world and those actions real for yourself, even if they are unfamiliar, you will find yourself naturally transformed into a new state of being. Acting is, in this way, not so much self-*expression* as it is self-*discovery* and self-*expansion*. This exploration of new ways of being is the most exciting aspect of the actor's creative process. It is why many actors greatly enjoy playing characters who are in some important way quite different from themselves.

The process whereby you come to inhabit the role is called *personalization*, and there are a number of techniques and concepts that can assist you in doing so with respect for the specific demands of the material. This will be the business of this step.

Needs and Personalization

As you now know, your character's behavior, like your own behavior in everyday life, is driven by needs. One of the best ways to personalize the character, to make it your own, is to identify the character's needs and to experience them for yourself, or to find analogous needs in your own experience that you can apply to the playing of the character.

We come to understand a character's needs through his or her actions. Actors sometimes make the mistake of trying to "play" needs: They try to *show* us how much they need self-esteem, how much they need to be loved, and so on. But as you already know, this results in *indicating*—that is, *showing* instead of *doing*. Trust that the writer has constructed the character so that his or her actions spring naturally from his or her needs, and you will begin to experience those needs as you begin to commit yourself to those actions.

For example, when Willy Loman flatters Howard's recording, we sense that the flattery is not genuine and that some subtext is at work—that is, Willy is using the flattery to gain some other, hidden objective. It is not difficult to deduce that Willy's need is to get Howard's favorable attention, and to understand further that this immediate need is connected directly to his scene objective of getting a spot in town, which in turn is connected to his superobjective of proving himself a worthy human being by being a successful salesman.

In fact, the most basic step in personalizing the character is to personalize his or her deepest overall need, their superobjective. Because the superobjective of most major characters is fairly universal, it is usually not difficult to personalize it. Like Willy Loman, we all want self-esteem, to be thought of as worthy, and thus we can all identify with Willy, however much we can see that Willy's way of pursuing self-esteem is mistaken.

Usually the superobjective reveals itself only gradually as you accumulate experiences of the character's needs beat by beat and scene by scene. A pattern begins to emerge that leads you to an understanding of the deeper need expressed through all these individual needs. Nevertheless, it can be useful to form a general idea of the superobjective from your early readings of the play; this initial idea can help guide and inspire your rehearsal exploration, though you know that it is temporary and subject to later specification and revision.

It may be more difficult to describe the superobjective of minor characters, because the writer has not provided much information about them. Here you can be inventive, so long as your understanding of the character enables you to accurately serve his or her dramatic function and keeps your performance in its proper perspective.

EXERCISE 9.1 **NEEDS**

1. Examine the entire play from which your scene comes: Does your character have some deep-seated, overall need that drives his or her actions throughout the play (a superobjective?)
2. How does this one overall need manifest itself within your scene? What are the immediate and specific needs driving each of your character's actions within this scene?
3. Do you have needs that are similar to those of your character? Can you begin to imagine yourself in the character's place, needing the same or analogous things?

Emotion Recall and Substitution

If you encounter a character whose needs or circumstances are so unfamiliar that you have difficulty experiencing them, you might try two techniques designed to help you connect material from your own life to your work. These techniques are *emotion recall* and *substitution*.

Stanislavski experimented with the idea that an actor could develop a wealth of emotion memories as a resource for the acting process, much as a painter learns to mix colors:

> The broader your emotion memory, the richer your material for inner creativeness....Our creative experiences are vivid and full in direct proportion to the power, keenness and exactness of our memory....Sometimes memories continue to live in us, grow and become deeper. They even stimulate new processes and either fill out unfinished details or suggest altogether new ones.[1]

There are several techniques by which stored memories may be recalled. One is *visualization*, which involves relaxing deeply and imagining yourself in the character's world, with all its sights, sounds, smells, physical sensations, and all the feelings and needs it involves. From these imagined experiences, you can invite associations from your store of personal memories to arise. These associations, or *recalls*, automatically become attached to the character's actions and situation in your understanding of them. It is neither necessary nor desirable to "play" them; simply allow them to influence you. The key to this technique is relaxation. When we relax, our storehouse of memory and subconscious material becomes more accessible. You may notice that when you do relaxation exercises such as meditation, or as you are falling asleep, memories often naturally flood in.

Another technique that may be useful in certain situations involves making a mental *substitution* of some situation or person from your own life

---

[1]Constantin Stanislavski, *An Actor's Handbook*, trans. and ed. Elizabeth Reynolds Hapgood (New York: Theatre Arts Books, 1936), p. 56. Copyright © 1936, 1961, 1963 by Elizabeth Reynolds Hapgood.

for the situation or character in the scene. If, for example, you are expected to be terribly afraid of another character, it might be useful to recall some frightening person from your own life and substitute that person in your own mind for the other character. Such a substitution will often arise naturally as you form associations between the world of the character and your own experience.

Of course, such emotion recalls and substitutions need not be rooted in real events; fantasy sometimes supplies more powerful material than does real life. Your dreams and imagination already provide a storehouse of situations and characters that are as useful in your acting as anything from your real life.

A word of caution: As useful as emotion recalls and substitutions may sometimes be, they must be used with discretion. For one thing, personal memories may be so powerful as to overwhelm artistic control. For another, recalls and substitutions can become *obstacles between you and your scene partners*; it is awful to be on stage with someone who is looking at you with a vacant stare because he or she is "seeing" someone else in his or her own mind or is busy reliving the day the family dog died. Finally, and most dangerous, recalls may distract you from your focus on your objective and may lure you into *playing an emotional state*. For all these reasons, recalls and substitutions may be carefully used as homework and perhaps even in early rehearsal, but are absolutely *not* intended for use in performance. Stanislavski himself eventually abandoned these techniques entirely.

EXERCISE 9.2 **RECALLS**

1. Place yourself comfortably at rest, and take a few deep breaths to relax.
2. Now go through your scene mentally; picture the entire circumstance, and live through your character's actions as if you were actually doing them in those circumstances. Let your body respond freely.
3. As you live through the scene in your mind, notice the emotional associations that arise. Do you remember events from your past? Do the other characters remind you of people you have known? Let yourself relive these memories fully.
4. Review this exercise, and evaluate any connections that were made. Are they useful to the scene? Do they need to be altered to meet the exact demands of the scene?
5. Perform your scene. Allow these associations to influence you, but avoid indicating them.
6. After your performance, discuss it with the group. Were you able to endow your character's need, situation, and action with personal significance? Did the character seem more real to the group? Are you beginning to feel a transformation into the character?

Entering The Character's Mind

Let's review our basic premise about how action flows in a scene; think back to the Impulse Circle exercise (7.1). The slap you received was a **stimulus**—it aroused you, caused a *reaction* as it passed through you, and then left you as an *action* as you slapped the next person's hand. Your action then became a stimulus for the next person and generated a reaction from them, which in turn generated another action, and so the slap moved around the circle. Similarly, a dramatic scene moves as the characters react to and act with one another, producing the flow of action–reaction–action–reaction that moves the scene forward.

Note that the energy leaving each character as action at any given moment in a scene is not the same as the energy that enters as stimulus; it is altered by the character's needs, personality, and objectives. So in a scene on stage, the "slap" is continually changing as the story evolves, which makes it more interesting and suspenseful.

From this, you can see that each character is a channel through which the energy of the story flows and that each character contributes something special to the changing nature of that energy as the story unfolds. *The inner process of reaction of each character is designed to produce the proper effect on each link of the reaction–action flow of the scene.* In rehearsal, you discover and experience what happens inside your character, moment by moment, as his or her reaction to a stimulus turns into an action directed toward an objective. Gradually, these discoveries accumulate and naturally begin to move you toward transformation.

It will be important, then, to understand and experience fully the internal process that leads to an action. When we examine it in detail, we see that it consists of several steps. These are represented graphically in Figure 9.1. In this figure, the large circle represents the boundary between the character's inner world and his or her outer world. As an example, we can apply the process shown in the drawing to the moment in *Death of a Salesman* when Willy enters and sees Howard playing with the recorder. Imagine yourself in Willy's place: The stimulus enters you through perception as you see and hear Howard playing with the recorder. This arouses a response in you that carries some **attitude**—it may excite or frighten or please or anger you, or some mixture of these. At this point, you might have an automatic (habitual) reaction that bypasses conscious thought, like blurting something out or knocking on something to demand Howard's attention. But you are too good a salesman to let impulse, even if you feel it strongly, rule you. Instead, you consider what you might do. We call this your *deliberation*. You have several alternatives; you might simply do nothing (suppression) and wait for Howard to finish with the recorder, but your need is too great for that; instead, you choose to use the recorder to advantage to ingratiate yourself to Howard by praising it. This is your **strategic choice**: Thus, *praising the recorder in order to gain Howard's favor* becomes your *action*, directed toward your *objective*, which is to ingratiate yourself to Howard and thereby get his favorable attention.

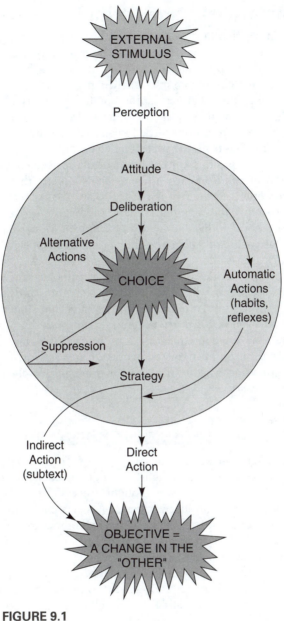

FIGURE 9.1
The Inner Process of Action

By fully reliving this inner phase of your character's action, you will most effectively enter into the character's mind. Let's explore each step of this process in detail.

Perception, Arousal, and Attitude

The process of inner action must begin with real perception, that is, real hearing and seeing. Although this seems obvious, some actors only pretend to hear or see what is said or done to them; they fear that if they let the other characters truly affect them, they will lose control of their performance. Instead of trusting and opening up to the other actors, they prefer the safety of reacting only to their own idea of what they want the other characters to say and do. It is as if they are responding to a prerecorded image of the other actor inside their own heads. When this happens, the performance becomes false and mechanical. Don't let fear turn you into this kind of hermetically sealed actor.

Actors have to depend on each other to provide what they and the scene need moment by moment to move the story forward as a real human event. Each actor must supply the required stimuli, and each must truly receive the stimuli provided. Although this doesn't always happen, we strive to achieve this ideal working relationship of real giving and taking. Remember: Acting is not so much doing things as it is allowing yourself to be *made* to do them. *Real acting is real reacting!* As you work, ask yourself, Am I really hearing and seeing my partner, or am I anticipating what I want him or her to say or do?

Once we are aroused, it is human nature to try to do something that will resolve the arousal, even if it is to try to ignore the arousal by suppressing it (a strategy that often has dire consequences, as in the case of Hamlet). But whether suppressed or not, the arousal energizes us, and we are motivated to take further action through either unconscious or conscious processes. Psychologists call this the need for *homeostasis*.

Deliberation and Strategic Choice

In Figure 9.1 you see that some arousals generate an automatic or habitual response that bypasses conscious thought, as we discussed in Step 6. If an action is not automatic, however, a conscious thought process begins. The first step in this conscious process is to consider various things you might do. As a result of this *deliberation*, one course of action is chosen, and others are rejected. In order to fully experience this process, it may be useful to understand the alternative choices that your character rejects. These can only be implied by the writer, and you must flesh them out for yourself. In other words, it may be as important for you to decide what your character chooses *not* to do as it is to know what he or she *does*.; after all, you can't really live through a choice unless you have real alternatives from which to choose. This can be your own special way of personalizing the character's inner world and can help you fully experience each choice your character makes.

Having deliberated the alternatives, your character—like people in everyday life—makes the choice that he or she thinks has the best chance for success given the circumstances. We call this a *strategic* choice. For example, in *Death of a Salesman*, Willy finds Howard playing with his recorder and as a seasoned salesman uses it to get his "foot in the door" by feigning interest in it.

This strategy seems like the best chance to achieve Willy's real objective, to get Howard's favorable attention so he can ask for a spot in town.

Follow the overall flow of energy in Figure 9.1. Notice that *strategic choice* is at the center of the entire inner process. Before the choice, energy is moving *into* you; after the choice, energy is moving *out* of you. Action, then, consists of two phases; the *instroke* of reaction leading to a *choice* which turns into an *outstroke* of action. In other words, *choice is the point at which reaction turns into action*—the essence of drama. The most suspenseful moments in stories occur when a character confronts a significant and difficult choice and we wonder, What will he or she do?

Choice is the most revealing and expressive point in the process of action. In the making of significant choices, your character is influenced by his or her needs, ways of seeing the world, relationships, beliefs, and values. *If you can experience all the factors influencing your character's most significant choices, you will be in touch with everything needed to create the character's mind.*

Your experience of your character's significant choices is also the main way the Magic If produces transformation in you. When you have entered into your character's circumstances and felt his or her needs, and then have truly lived through his or her choices, action will follow naturally, and with it will come transformation.

The Inner Monologue

Experiencing the process whereby your character forms his or her actions is the most important step toward transformation. Here is a good general rule: Whatever your character *doesn't* need to think about (their automatic actions) ideally should become automatic or spontaneous for you as well; whatever your character *does* need to think about (their strategic choices), you must also think through each and every time you rehearse or perform the scene.

As another detailed example of this process of inner action, consider the exchange between Amanda and Laura from a scene in *The Glass Menagerie*. Amanda has just discovered that her daughter has not been going to her classes at a business college because she became so nervous in class that she threw up; ashamed to tell her mother, Laura has been pretending to continue with school while actually walking in the park every day. In Amanda's world, there are only three choices available to young single women: a business career, marriage, or spinsterhood. Since Laura's chances for a career seem hopeless, Amanda decides that the next best chance is to find some nice young man for Laura to marry—a gentleman caller like the ones she herself entertained in her youth in the old south. She jumps up and announces her plan to Laura. Amanda's inner thought process at this point might flow like this:

1. *Stimulus.* The only alternative is marriage! To some nice man! Of course!
2. *Attitude.* But I'll have to take charge, or nothing will happen.
3. *Alternatives.* She has no gentlemen callers the way I did. How can we find one?

4. *Choice.* Tom must know lots of nice young men down at the shoe factory. I'll order him to bring one home!

5. *Action.* Announcing the decision to Laura.

6. *Objective.* To rally Laura to the plan.

When Laura hears her mother's idea, she is terrified. Because of her limp, she considers herself crippled and unattractive to men. She reaches for her glass animal and goes over to the photograph of her father; these are automatic actions, things she does every time she feels threatened—a retreat into her "safe" illusory world. But she also tries to deal with the situation in a conscious way, and her internal thought process might flow like this:

1. *Stimulus.* Married? Can she really be thinking that?

2. *Attitude.* No one would want to marry me—I'm a cripple.

3. *Alternatives.* I could just hide (*reaching for the glass animal*). Or maybe I could run away, the way father did (*going to the photograph*).

4. *Choice.* No, I've got to talk her out of it.

5. *Action.* Reminding Amanda that she is crippled.

6. *Objective.* To make mother see that her plan is impossible.

You can see that Amanda's and Laura's needs, values, way of thinking, sense of self, way of relating to the world—in short, their entire psychology—is involved and expressed in each step of their mental processes. Notice, too, how Tennessee Williams has provided physical actions (Amanda getting up and Laura going to the animals and photograph) that externalize the inner thought processes of both characters.

Giving words to the internal thought process in the way we just did is called creating an **inner monologue.** Purposefully creating such a detailed inner monologue as part of your preparation for a role can help you to specify and experience your understanding of your character's thought process. In performance, this thought process will once again become intuitive and nearly instantaneous.

Such a highly detailed view of your character's inner thought process may be useful for highly significant choices, but it is too cumbersome to use on a moment-by-moment basis. We will simplify the process by breaking it into three basic steps: The first step, which we will call simply *reaction,* contains the stimulus, need, and attitude; the second step is *choice* and includes the consideration of alternatives and the choice of a strategic action; finally, the external activity directed toward the chosen objective is the *action.* So your inner process can be summarized by three key words:

reaction–choice–action

This can also be seen as **instroke-choice-outstroke** since before the choice the energy is flowing into you as reaction, and after the choice your energy is flowing out of you as action.

In general, actors are naturally attracted to the outstroke, to what they *do;* but they are often deficient in experiencing the instroke, what it is that *makes* them do. When we think about *motivation* (what makes us do things) we should remember that motivation turns into *aspiration* (what we want) and that it is only the entire process whereby action is formed that provides a complete experience of the character's mind.

You can apply this system by asking yourself three questions about each of the transactions in a scene:

1. What am I reacting to?
2. What does it make me want?
3. What do I do to try to get it?

EXERCISE 9.3   INNER MONOLOGUE

1. Answer the three questions above about each of your character's actions in your scene.
2. Choose the most significant choice your character makes in the scene, and examine it in detail. Create the inner monologue that expresses your character's mental process for this choice. Try writing down the inner monologue.
3. Rehearse your scene with your partner. Take the time to experience each choice fully.
4. Perform the scene for your group, and discuss it. Were the moments of choice clear and believable?

The Super-Choice

In an entire role, there may be one singular choice that stands out above all the rest, and identifying this *super-choice* and understanding the factors, both internal and external, that influence it can provide guidance of great importance in creating the role. The super-choice is the moment at which the character's superobjective is most manifested. For example, in *The Glass Menagerie*, Tom's super-choice is to leave home for good. This choice is made at the height of a terrible argument with his mother in which she blames him for the failure of her fantasy that Jim the Gentleman Caller will become a husband for Laura. Jim realizes at that moment that he can never fulfill Amanda's dreams, that there will never be a place for him in the house (spatially or emotionally), and that if he stays he must sacrifice all his own dreams. Every other choice Tom makes throughout the play leads him to this choice, and so the actor can understand how the action in each scene must be shaped to lead to this moment.

EXERCISE 9.4   THE SUPER-CHOICE

1. Considering the entire play, is there a single choice your character makes that stands out above all the rest? Especially one that affects his or her eventual fate?
2. Examine this choice and consider both the internal and the external factors that affect it.

3. What can you learn from this analysis that will guide you in making the choices your character makes in all the other scenes? Can you see a through-line forming that leads to this choice?
4. What does this tell you about the qualities your character most needs to have?

Autobiography, Diary, and Self-Image

Three good ways to inspire your exploration of your character's inner and outer worlds is by writing an autobiography and a diary entry for them and exploring their self-image. These are techniques that can be used in the middle phase of rehearsals, after you have had a chance to experience some of your character's specific thought processes and actions. They are a good way to crystallize your developing understanding of the character.

EXERCISE 9.5   **AUTOBIOGRAPHY AND DIARY**

1. Imagine that as your character, you have been asked to write a short autobiographical sketch of yourself; limit yourself to two pages and include only those things that were most influential in your life; title your essay, "The Things Which Made Me Who I Am."
2. As your character, write a diary entry for the day on which your scene occurs. Begin with them waking up and follow them through the details of their day leading up to the beginning of the scene itself.

Consider also how your character sees himself or herself. Self-image is often a self-fulfilling prophecy; for example, if Willy Loman's superobjective is to prove himself worthy by earning money and respect, his underlying self-image must be that he is *un*worthy, and much of his behavior seems perversely dedicated to proving his own unworthiness. Here is an exercise in self-image that can inspire your participation in the mind of your character.

EXERCISE 9.6   **SELF-IMAGE**

1. Relax, enter into your character's frame of mind, and complete these phrases:
   a. The most beautiful part of my body is…
   b. Happiness to me is…
   c. The thing I most want to do before I die is…
   d. The ugliest part of my body is…
   e. The thing I like best about myself is…
   f. Pain to me is…
   g. My mother…
   h. The most secret thing about me is…
   i. I hear my father's voice speaking through my own when I tell myself…
   j. Love to me is…

     k. If you could hear the music in me...
     l. I want my epitaph to be...
  2. Now, immediately work through the scene, and allow these feelings to affect you.

Again, avoid the temptation to indicate. It is never your aim to explain your character to the audience; your job is to create experience, not to explain behavior.

Summary of Step 9

An important part of your job is to personalize the character's needs, putting yourself in his or her place. There are several techniques that can help in this effort, such as recalling emotional experiences or substituting relationships from your own life. These techniques may be part of your personal preparation, but they are *not* meant to be used in performance because they may distance you from the scene and your partners.

The internal process by which conscious action is formed looks like this: You perceive a stimulus that arouses you and generates an attitude, which prompts either an automatic reaction that bypasses conscious choice or a consideration of alternatives, which leads to a strategic choice of an action directed toward an objective. The chosen action may be direct, indirect, or suppressed. By fully reliving this inner phase of action, you will most effectively enter into your character's mind.

Strategic choice is at the center of the entire inner process; before the choice, energy is moving into you; after the choice, energy is moving out of you. Because choice is the moment at which reaction turns into action, it is the essence of drama. Your inner process can be summarized by three key words: reaction–choice–action.

Experiencing the process whereby your character forms his or her actions is the most important step toward transformation. Whatever your character *doesn't* need to think about ideally should become automatic or spontaneous for you as well; whatever your character *does* need to think about, you must also think through each and every time you perform the scene. Giving words to an internal thought process is called creating an inner monologue.

In an entire role, there may be one singular choice that stands out above all the rest, and identifying this *super-choice* and understanding the factors, both internal and external, that influence it can provide guidance of great importance in creating the role.

Three good ways to focus your developing experience of the character is by writing an autobiography and a diary entry for them and exploring their self-image.

PART THREE

The Performance and After

In Part 1 you began to prepare yourself by learning to relax, center yourself, and activate your body, voice, and speech. In Part 2 you developed an understanding of the importance of reactions, choice, objectives and actions, as well as the way scenes work and are shaped for dramatic impact through the operation of beats and crisis, how to connect your character's inner process to the scene, and the foundations of character. Here in Part 3 you will follow the steps by which a play is rehearsed and staged, and begin to prepare your own scene for performance.

You would normally have the benefit of a director's guidance during this stage of the work, but for class purposes you will rely on the feedback from your teacher and your fellow students. If at all possible, arrange for a "public" showing of your scene at the end of the process; this will give you an experience of the kind of energy an impending performance provides. A showing for other students and faculty in your department would be an ideal format.

STEP 10

Early Rehearsals

LEARNING OBJECTIVES

- Distinguish the steps by which an actual performance is created, beginning with auditions and the early stages of rehearsal such as table readings, memorization of lines, and first experiments in finding the physical and vocal aspects of the emerging character.
- Outline the qualities that make for good communication and working habits in rehearsal, with special emphasis of your relationship with your director.

Although there are various ways in which individual directors may choose to structure the rehearsal process, the typical sequence has ten steps, some of which go on simultaneously. From the actor's point of view, they are as follows:

1. Auditions and casting
2. Actor preparation and homework
3. Early readings
4. Getting up and off book
5. Exploring the action
6. Blocking and staging
7. Establishing the score, pacing and polishing the performance
8. Technical and dress rehearsals
9. Opening

Auditions

Though not usually thought of as part of the rehearsal process, auditions are in fact a time when you may form an initial approach to a role that will greatly influence your later work.

Auditions are a nerve-wracking, but necessary, part of the actor's life. If it is any consolation to you, directors are also under tremendous pressure during auditions; the casting of a play is usually the most important decision the director will have to make, and yet this often has to be done with only superficial knowledge of the actors.

In general we can divide auditions into two types, the "general" and the "specific." Most general auditions, sometimes called "cattle calls," are used for preliminary screening for a role, or for membership in a company, or admission to a training program. In this type of audition, you are often asked to present two monologues of different types within a certain time limit. For this purpose you should develop a repertoire of at least four carefully chosen and prepared monologues, including comedy and tragedy and poetic and modern styles. About two minutes is a good length for each, though some might be as short as one minute. Beware of going on too long; it is much better to make a strong initial impression and leave the auditioners hungry for more.

Your repertoire of speeches should be chosen to demonstrate your abilities to the best advantage, but most important, they should be material that you love; it will be a tremendous advantage to you if your positive feelings for your material outweigh your negative feelings about auditioning. You should be glad to have a chance to share this wonderful material with the auditioners.

At the audition itself, introduce yourself and your selections clearly and in a businesslike way, making direct and pleasant eye contact with the auditioners. Dress neatly and appropriately to the material you will perform, but not in a "costume." Take time to prepare yourself and the space, but work efficiently. Your focus should be on the work itself; let your appetite for acting motivate you.

Provide a well-organized and attractive resume, and an 8×10 photo; black and white was once traditional, but today many auditioners prefer color. This "**head shot**" will assist the auditioners in remembering you; it should be current, attractive, and "neutral"; that is, it should look like you and not limit the impression it provides of you to one quality, like "sexy," "likeable," or "dangerous." Two copies of the photo are often requested. Your resume should be attached to the back of your photo.

Shape each speech in your audition to have a smooth, logical progression; this may require some judicious editing, and internal cutting is allowable. Make sure each piece has a satisfying ending, even if that is not how it would be performed in context. This will show the auditioners that you have a desire to satisfy an audience and respect for a well-shaped performance.

In monologues where another character is assumed to be present, be careful to "create" the other person by the way you relate to them; place them (in your mind) somewhere just off center (not off to one side) a bit closer to you than the auditioners. Do not look directly at the auditioners during the performance unless the speech is intended by the author as direct address.

When the audition is for a specific role, you will usually be given a scene, or part of a scene, to read, often opposite a stage manager or casting assistant. Although you should try to read the entire play in advance, this is usually not possible. (In the professional theater, union rules require that a copy of the entire play must be made available to you.) In actual practice, you will usually receive a copy of the material in advance (from your agent, if you have one) and will report for the audition at a certain time a day or two later. Given this limited time to prepare for the audition, your immediate task is to find a productive objective and playable action in the material, and to make that objective important to you through some kind of personalization. Use the principles you learned in Part 2.

Perhaps the greatest challenge in an audition is to allow yourself to really be in the here and now. Usually, your nervousness about the audition will make you come away from it with only a vague sense of what happened or who was there; try instead to be present and aware. Take a moment at the beginning to breathe, to see where you are and who is there; treat it like a social situation in which you are glad to be present. The auditioners are eager to get some idea of what kind of person and worker you are.

Then, as you perform, go for it. Make the event live. If the material is not memorized, don't be tied to your script (but don't ignore it completely). It is better to be a bit rough on the lines but alive, than to be technically correct but mechanical.

Auditions are much more enjoyable if you approach them without a sense of competitiveness. Think of them not as a contest with other actors but as an opportunity to communicate your potential to a director or producer. Take the long view and remember that the opinion formed of you at an audition may be important at some future time; it is therefore important that you honestly present your best abilities and avoid falsifying yourself for the sake of the particular instance. The question young actors most often ask about an audition is, "What do they want?" A much better question would be, "How can I best show them what kind of actor I am?" It is important to communicate your love for acting and your discipline and craftsmanship; one of the first things a director asks himself or herself about an actor in an audition is usually, "is this someone I want to work with?"

Above all, do not take auditions personally. It usually requires many auditions before you will land a part. You can't take every rejection as a reflection on your talent. Auditions do not test your artistry so much as they test your usefulness for the specific role at hand. True, once you are cast you will have to deliver the goods, but to be cast in the first place you have to be in the right place at the right time.

EXERCISE 10.1   AUDITIONS

Set up a general audition situation in your class. Each of you is to present two monologues, one modern and one classical. They should be no more than a total of three minutes in total: a timekeeper will stop you when your time is up. After each audition, the class critiques the work.

Preparation and Homework

Once you have been cast in a role, you will do some important preparation on your own before rehearsals begin, and indeed your "homework" will continue throughout the entire rehearsal process. Analysis, private experimentation, learning lines, and private rehearsal of special skills must be accomplished outside the rehearsal hall. Never should you waste the time of your fellow actors and director by failing to do your homework.

Remember that homework is a *preparation* for rehearsal, not a substitute for it. Your prerehearsal work identifies the possibilities that will then be explored in rehearsal with your fellow actors; it does *not* determine the form of the finished product. Unfortunately, some actors are so insecure that they prepare for rehearsal as if it were performance, creating a rigidly premeditated form; the director then must be a "referee," mediating between the various actors' ideas of how to play their roles. Remember that rehearsal is a time for *mutual* exploration through trial and error.

Depending on the demands of the material, your preparation may take various forms. You will certainly examine the play as a whole, and develop a preliminary sense of your character's dramatic function, and even begin to form a provisional sense of your superobjective. You might also do a preliminary breakdown of your scenes, dividing them into beats, forming an idea of where the crises occur, and developing a preliminary sense of your beat and scene objectives.

There may be technical demands on your voice or body related to the specific role that will require a good deal of homework; for example, Laurence Olivier devoted a full year to his vocal preparation for Othello. Besides technical preparations of vocal and physical skills related to the external behavior of the character, you will also want to prepare yourself to enter the character's mind, as in Step 9. For this purpose you may need to do research into the world from which the character comes; you will be most interested in those things that established the character's psychological and moral qualities, such as the religious and philosophical beliefs of the time, the educational experiences of the character, the quality of his or her home life, the work environment of the time, the system of government and justice, and so on.

You might also need to develop certain technical skills related to the style of the production, such as fencing, dancing, tumbling, the use of canes, fans, large skirts, or robes, and so on. For period plays especially, you may want to do some research into the fashions of the time, the ideas of grace, beauty, and social behavior. Experiencing the music, painting, and architecture of the time is valuable; documents such as diaries, letters, and newspapers can also be helpful.

EXERCISE 10.2 HOMEWORK

Examine your scene for each of the following, and plan a program of homework that will prepare you for each:

1. Any stylistic or historical qualities of the play that you need to know more about
2. Any meanings or other qualities of the language that you need to understand; prepare a paraphrase as in Step 5
3. Any skills or qualities of the character that you must practice so that they become habitual
4. Forming a preliminary sense of the structure of the scene by making a breakdown of the beats and crisis

Early Read-Throughs

As rehearsals begin and you are meeting for the first time with your fellow cast members, your director may start things off in a variety of ways: some will outline their interpretation and approach to the play; some will lead a discussion about it; some may do exercises to "break the ice" and to establish a working rapport in the ensemble; others will dispense with any such preliminaries and begin at once to read the play.

These early "table" readings are your first forays into the heart of the material. Begin to work at once on the play as a whole; listen to it in the actual voices of your fellow actors and begin to discover how the play will live within this particular group of people. Above all, read in relationship, with a spirit of give-and-take, and get your awareness and your eyes out of your book as much as you can and contact the other characters in your scenes. Read in a dramatic rather than a literary mode. Begin to search for the action that lives only in the specific transactions between the characters. Read also with deep muscle involvement even though you are sitting at a table, so that you involve your whole self; you will find that a wealth of associations and ideas well up.

These early rehearsals are exploration, but never indiscriminate exploration. Any meaningful exploration has a sense of goal that prevents it from degenerating into blind groping. There is usually in the vision of a play as communicated by the director some sense of the direction in which your exploration must go.

Not all of your rehearsal discoveries will result from purposeful experimentation, of course; the accidental is an important part of any creative process. You must have the courage to be playful, to invite the "happy accident" to happen, and to benefit from it. Such spontaneous discovery grows best from the receptiveness and responsiveness of each cast member to each other and to the moment. In these early stages of rehearsal, as rapport is being established within the company, it is especially important that each actor make an act of faith to work together toward the defining of goals with respect, trust, good humor, and a generous heart.

EXERCISE 10.3   **TABLE READING**

Sit with your partner at a table and read the scene together; practice getting your focus out of the book and onto one another, and reading with a strong sense of the give-and-take of the scene. Strive for total physical involvement even though you are seated.

Getting Up and Off Book

As soon as possible, you begin to put your book aside so that you can explore the action on your feet. This, of course, requires learning the lines. You will have to find your own best method for line memorization. Some actors like to have a friend read the other parts ("cue" them); some make a tape recording of their lines to listen to at night; some even write out their lines. Many find it useful to begin working in paraphrase, finding the ideas behind the lines in their own words first.

However you work, be sure to learn the *action* as well as the *lines*, that is, learn the words in the context of the give-and-take of the scene, paying considerable attention to what the other character is saying. This is not only an easier way of learning your lines, but it also makes learning them a useful first step in your exploration of the action. You will find that the more fully you understand your character's actions, the easier it will be to learn the lines that are driven by those actions.

The transitional period in the rehearsal process during which you are putting the book down and beginning to move can be a frustrating one. Understand that during this period it is expected that you will often have to call for lines. When you call for a line, do not waste time apologizing, and above all keep the action of the scene going while you call for the line *in character*. Simply say "line" when needed and someone assigned to be "on book" (usually the stage manager or an assistant) will supply the first few words of the next line. This is a necessary and unavoidable process during which it is important that you continue to play the scene and explore the action with your fellow actors.

During this period you may or may not be actually setting the movements (the *blocking*) of the scene, depending on the way your director chooses to work. Often, the groundplan of the set will have been established (and perhaps taped out on the floor of the rehearsal room) and you will move within it according to your own impulses; many directors like to allow the blocking to emerge gradually in this way. You will find that your lines are much easier to learn once they can be tied to physical movements.

For the scene you are working on for this book, you should by now be well on your way to having it memorized. *Subsequent exercises will require that you have your lines thoroughly memorized.* As soon as possible get completely off book; have someone serve as your stage manager and cue you as you rehearse.

EXERCISE 10.4   **GETTING OFF BOOK**

After you have both achieved a good level of memorization of your lines, have someone serve as a stage manager for you as you and your partner put your scripts down and start to go through the scene on your feet, calling for lines without apology, in character, and so as to keep the action of the scene moving. Don't concern yourself with blocking at this point; simply move according to your impulses.

Exploring the Character's Body

As you get off book and onto your feet, you will begin to experience the way the action affects the character's body, and the way the language of the play lives in the character's mouth. As rehearsals progress, you may begin to discover things about your character's body and voice that are required by the action of the play, or simply "feel right," and a rudimentary physical and vocal characterization may begin to form. Do not rush or force this process: These sorts of discoveries will occur naturally in the course of rehearsal and you must beware of self-consciously or intellectually imposing physical or vocal choices that become mere posing or affectations.

Many actors find this early bodily exploration useful in developing a fundamental experience of the character. In Step 2 you explored the sense of center within the body, and also the way you experience gravity from that center; now, your character's sense of center and experience of gravity can be fundamental aspects of these early physical explorations. For example, the great British actor Sir Alec Guinness felt that he had not yet found the basis of a character until he had found the proper *walk*, and indeed a character's walk identifies the character's center and sums up his or her relationship to gravity and attitude toward the world.

The Russian actor, director, and teacher, Michael Chekhov (1891–1955) knew that Stanislavsky's final development of his method as presented in his book *The Method of Physical Actions* used the mind–body connection to encourage a physical approach to character rather than an exclusively psychological one—in other words, by working from the outside in rather than strictly from the inside out. Chekhov used this idea to develop the technique of the **Psychological Gesture.** This is a single physical action that sums up the psychology of the character. The power of the psychological gesture (called simply the *PG* by devotees) is in the process of finding it and finally perfecting it; it is intended for your private use as a powerful trigger of your experience of the character, *not* as an element of the performance to be communicated to the audience.

Once you have developed the PG (usually in later stages of rehearsal), Chekhov believed that committing it puts you instantly into character, because in one movement it awakens the essence of the character in you, inspiring not only your walk, posture, and other physical and vocal qualities and mannerisms but also your thoughts and feelings. This technique is used today by many great actors such as Jack Nicholson, Anthony Hopkins, and Johnny Depp.

EXERCISE 10.5 **PHYSICAL EXPLORATION**

1. As you rehearse, watch for gestures and bodily configurations that evoke a strong sense of the character in you. Let them grow and develop. Use the technique you learned in Step 2 to explore the placement of the center of your character, as well as their relationship to gravity as expressed by their "root."
2. Gradually, this physical exploration may develop into a single psychological gesture that serves you as a trigger to enter the life of the character.

Communication in Rehearsals

As you now know, plays depend on the interactions between the characters. This means that your individual creation as an actor cannot be separated from the work of all the other actors and the director. As playwright August Strindberg observed:

No form of art is as dependent as the actor's. He cannot isolate his particular contribution, show it to someone and say, "This is mine." If he does not get the support of his fellow actors, his performance will lack resonance and depth... He won't make a good impression no matter how hard he tries. Actors must rely on each other...That is why rapport among actors is imperative for the success of a play. I don't care whether you rank yourselves higher or lower than each other, or from side to side, or from inside out—as long as you do it together.[1]

An effective rehearsal process therefore depends on good communication skills from all involved. Your working relationships will be most effective when they are based upon three principles: first, mutual commitment to the working relationship and to the work itself; second, mutual support for one another's individual objectives and methods; and third, free and open communication so that problems can be worked out and thereby become opportunities for creative interaction. Let's examine each.

First, you are *committed* to the working relationship because it will enable you to do better work as an individual. Friendship will result from most of your working relationships and there is a wonderfully warm sense of kinship among actors; often you meet another actor for the first time and because of your mutual friends you know at once that you are "family." But commitment to the working relationship is not necessarily the same thing as being "friends," and it is possible to work effectively with people you don't particularly like. Although group membership requires generosity, good humor, and a spirit of reasonable compromise, the need to be "nice" should never cause you to falsify your personal values or discipline. Remember: the group doesn't make good work because it is a good group; it becomes a good group because it creates good work.

Second, your *support* for one another's objectives and methods is the basis of respect. You might not share another actor's reasons for doing what they do, nor work the same way, but you respect their motives and their right to work in their own way, just as you expect respect for your motives and methods. If the differences in your ways of working cause a problem (as they sometimes do), negotiate compromises on both sides that, as much as possible, meet everyone's needs equally.

Finally, the possibility of free and open *communication* is critical. Problems arise in any creative process and they must be worked through and negotiated; only free and open communication will make that possible. Free and open communication does not mean that we say everything that's on our mind in the name of "honesty"; some things are best left unsaid—as Shakespeare's Falstaff says, "discretion is the better part of valor"—but the possibility of discussing problems needs to be felt by everyone. Otherwise an atmosphere of repression will develop and tensions will mount, perhaps to a boiling point.

---

[1]August Strindberg, "Notes to the Members of the Intimate Theatre," trans. Everett Sprinchorn, The Tulane Drama Review, 6 no. 2 (November 1961), p. 157. This material is also copyrighted by The Drama Review, 1967.

In addition to the group's need for good communication, you have an individual need for it as both an actor and as a student of acting. Actors depend on feedback more than most other artists; the notes you get from your teachers, directors, and fellow actors are tremendously important in guiding your growth. Actors therefore have a solemn responsibility to provide accurate and useful feedback to one another.

The most effective feedback we can give each other is based upon a few basic principles. Most important, *say what you see and how it makes you feel*. Don't say, "Why are you hiding," say, "I noticed that you rarely looked at your partner during this scene, and that made me feel as if you were hiding from us. What was going on?" Do you see the difference between these two statements? In the first statement, you interpreted the reason for what you saw, and then reported your interpretation as if it were true. In the second statement you reported your specific observation, and then reported the feeling it engendered in you without guessing at the cause; now you can go on to discuss the situation profitably.

Once you have an effective message to send, consider some effective ways of sending it:

1. Be CLEAR about your message before you deliver it.
2. Be SPECIFIC, SIMPLE, and DIRECT; use examples.
3. Pick an APPROPRIATE TIME to communicate.
4. CHECK to see if your message was received accurately.

Here is an exercise to practice these communication skills.

EXERCISE 10.6   ATTRACTIONS AND RESERVATIONS, AGONIES AND ECSTASIES

Join with your scene partner to share impressions of your own and each other's work. Take turns completing the following statements; be specific and direct; supply examples.

1. My greatest agony about my own work just now is…
2. The greatest reservation I have about your work is…
3. The thing I feel best about in my own work is…
4. The thing that attracts me most about your work is…

Compare your feelings about praise and criticism. Which do you take more seriously? Did you learn equally from each? Are you benefiting from the feedback of others enough? Or are you too dependent on them?

Unfortunately, despite the nature of their work, most actors have no better communication skills than most other people. Here is a list of the most common pitfalls in communication. Think back over your working experiences. Have you suffered from or been guilty of any of the following communication disorders?

1. Fogging: Using generalities without referring to specifics. Example: "You need to work on your voice."
2. Mind raping: Assuming you know what someone is thinking without bothering to check. Example: "Why are you hiding from us in this scene?"

3. Defusing: Excessive self-criticism that makes it impossible for anyone else to criticize you. Example: "I just couldn't concentrate at all today; I know the scene was terrible, but what did you think?"
4. Dumping: Using criticism as an emotional release or as a weapon.
5. Gunnysacking: Saving up grievances until an explosion becomes likely.
6. No trespassing: When unstated rules exist within a group that certain people or certain issues may not be criticized.
7. Holier-than-thou: Criticism of others for the purpose of avoiding criticism of self.
8. Doomsaying: Feedback that emphasizes only the negative without acknowledging the positive.

You and Your Director

The relationship between actor and director deserves special attention. Since the director is the focus of the group's working process, your ability to work effectively with your director is critical. It will help if you have a clear sense of what each of your functions, rights, and responsibilities are.

The director has four main functions: (1) to guide the development of an overall interpretation for the production; (2) to align the efforts of all the different artists contributing to the production; (3) to provide feedback during rehearsals by being "an ideal audience of one"; and (4) to establish a common approach to the conduct of rehearsals.

Each director has a characteristic way of working, and it is easier for the actors to adapt to the director's method than for the director to adopt an individual approach for each of the actors. It is therefore part of your job to adapt, as much as is reasonable, to the director's approach, and to help the director develop the most effective channel of communication with you.

The interpretive function makes the director a "central intelligence" for the production, establishing its point of view. He or she either provides this focus at the outset, or guides the cast in discovering it during rehearsals. Your performance, like every other element of the production, must be aligned toward this central interpretation. Even if your personal preference might be for a different interpretation or emphasis, once you have accepted the role, it is your job to work effectively within the director's production concept. In general, the director is the final authority on *what* and the actor is the final authority on *how*.

One bothersome attitude is that of the actor who becomes an apologist for his or her character, arguing from the character's point of view as if every scene "belonged to them." Group interpretation can be ruined by actors who insist upon adopting their character's point of view at the expense of the play as an artistic whole. On the other hand, we do a great disservice to our director, our fellow actors, and ourselves if, out of our desire to avoid conflict, we fail to express ourselves honestly. An actor who is too pliable is as destructive as one who is too rigid. Your ideas will be appreciated if they are presented in a reasoned, timely, and respectful fashion. While a show has only one director, everyone connected with it must feel responsible for the whole production, and provide any ideas that may be of value.

Above all, avoid directing your fellow actors. You express your needs or feelings about the work, but you do not try to instruct others in how to satisfy those needs. If problems with other actors persist, speak privately to your director and decide together on the best course of action.

There are many ways in which the responsibilities of director and actor overlap and compromise will be necessary. The actor, intimately involved with the life of the character, possesses insights into the life of that character that are denied to the director. At the same time, the director has an objective overview unavailable to the actor. In an effective working relationship, each will respect and value the insights and perspective of the other and seek to join their points of view to the best possible advantage.

Even in the best situations there are times when insoluble disagreements occur; when this happens, ties go to the director. The director has assumed public responsibility for the interpretation of the production, while you have assumed public responsibility only for the portrayal of your character within the context established by that interpretation. Once the director's interpretation has been clarified, it is your responsibility to find the best possible means of implementing it.

To sum up, you and your director are coworkers, not master and slave. Though you share many responsibilities, you have essentially different functions that are interdependent and equal. The director's responsibility is to the overall production concept, and your responsibility is to bring your role to life so as to best contribute to that concept.

Summary of Step 10

As nerve wracking as they are, auditions are a time when you often form an initial approach to a role. For general auditions you should develop a repertoire of at least four prepared audition pieces chosen to demonstrate your abilities to the best advantage, preferably material that you love.

When given a scene in order to audition for a specific role, your immediate job is to find a productive objective and playable action in the material and to make the objective important to you. In the audition itself, allow yourself to be in the here and now; make the event live. Make contact with the person you are performing with (even if imaginary) and try to affect them. Take the long view and remember that the opinion formed of you at an audition may be important at some future time. Think "how can I best show them what kind of actor I am?"

Once cast, you begin your preparation: analysis, beginning to learn the lines, and private rehearsal of special skills must be accomplished outside the rehearsal hall. Remember that homework is a preparation for rehearsal, not a substitute for it.

At the first readings, begin at once to search for the action that lives in the transactions between the characters; read in relationship, with a spirit of give-and-take. Even though you are seated, read with complete physical involvement.

As soon as possible, put your book aside so that you can explore the action on your feet. Keep the action going while you call for lines in character without apology.

As rehearsals progress, a rudimentary physical and vocal characterization may begin to form. The technique of the *psychological gesture* the development of a single physical action that sums up the psychology of the character, may be useful.

Your working relationships will be most effective when they are based upon three principles: mutual commitment to the working relationship and to the work itself; mutual support for one another's individual objectives and methods; and free and open communication so that problems can be thrashed out and thereby become opportunities for creative interaction. Communication is more effective when it is simple, clear, and direct.

You and your director are coworkers, not master and slave. The director's first responsibility is to the overall patterning of the play as a theatrical experience; your responsibility is to bring your role to life so as to best contribute to that pattern.

STEP 11

Staging and Final Rehearsals

LEARNING OBJECTIVES

- Consider the implications for your performance of various kinds of stages, such as proscenium, three-quarter and full-round, and environmental.
- Master the vocabulary of stage movement and experience how, as performance nears, you begin to establish a reliable and repeatable score that underlies the performance on a fundamental level.
- Experience the impact in the final weeks of the addition of the physical elements of setting, lighting, costumes, and props during technical and dress rehearsals.

As you prepare your scene for final performance, you must consider what adjustments may be needed to make your work accessible to an audience. Your first consideration will be the physical and vocal adjustments required by the theatrical space in which you will perform. Since we often prepare performances in rehearsal halls that are not necessarily the same size as the stage and auditorium in which we will perform, and since economic pressures usually restrict the amount of time we will have to move the production into the actual performance space, we must consider the demands of that space in advance as part of our preparation.

Types of Stages

A stage is defined by its spatial relationship to the audience. There are four basic types of stage configurations: proscenium, thrust, arena, and environmental (see Figure 11.1). Let's consider how each of these basic types impacts an actor.

118

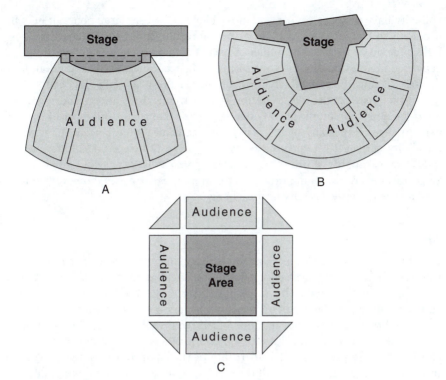

FIGURE 11.1

Types of Stages: (A) Traditional proscenium; (B) Modern thrust; (C) Arena

Proscenium

The traditional proscenium stage features an arch through which the audience sees the action. This "picture frame" evolved as a way of establishing a point of reference for settings painted in perspective (hence, the word "proscenium," which means "in front of the scene"). An actor on a proscenium stage must, of course, realize that the audience is limited to one side of the playing area. In realistic plays on proscenium stages, the walls of the set and the placement of furniture are usually splayed open to audience view, creating a somewhat artificial environment. It will be your job to play within this artificial space so as to create the entire environment, including the invisible "fourth wall" that separates audience and stage.

Some directors and actors think that, like the set and furniture, actors must also **cheat out** (turn their bodies partly out toward the audience), but this is not as necessary as some think. Excessive cheating out makes characters look as if they are more interested in relating to the audience than to one another, so although you may make some adjustments because of the audience's location, you must do so without destroying the logic of the character's relationships. Don't underestimate how much acting you can do with your back.

Depending on the size of the house, the proscenium may require an adjustment in the overall **scale** of the performance. In order to be heard and seen well, you may have to speak louder and move bigger. In a very large house, it may be necessary to increase your volume when you turn upstage, since stage sets rarely reflect the voice back to the audience well. You may even have to find ways to deliver your lines downstage toward the audience, especially in many outdoor theaters such as those in which most summer Shakespeare festivals occur.

In the past few decades there has been a tremendous advance in the quality and subtlety of amplification systems for the live stage, and most of today's performances (especially of musicals) are electronically enhanced. As a result, the ability of the actor to project seems less important nowadays, and few actors today are as capable of projecting in large spaces as were previous generations. Since vocal energy is an important factor in any performance, however, volume may not be the only casualty of this change.

Thrust

The thrust stage (so called because it "thrusts" into the midst of the audience) features the same stage/audience relationship as that found in classical Greek and Elizabethan theaters. This stage places the actor in close proximity to the audience and limits the use of scenery, so it is very much an actor's theater.

The thrust stage has not just one but three invisible walls; there is usually scenery at the rear and furniture or objects arranged throughout the stage, so you will have to play the full 360° reality of the environment while striving to stay open to audience view on all three sides, or at least to distribute your presence equally to all sections of the house. It is especially important on a thrust stage for you and your fellow actors to stand farther apart than usual; if you are too close, you will block one another from audience view and will throw shadows on one another's faces. The increased sense of audience contact inherent in the thrust stage requires a more detailed and subtle performance than on most proscenium stages.

Arena

The arena and other types of full-round stages stand at the opposite extreme from proscenium stages. Here the audience surrounds the stage and all four walls are invisible, though doorways and windows are sometimes indicated by physical elements. The arena stage offers the greatest sense of intimacy of all stage types and is usually relatively small. Audiences tend to expect an even more detailed and subtle performance here than in other kinds of theaters, something closer to what is required for film acting. The completeness of the performance helps to compensate for the fact that an actor's back is always to some part of the audience.

Environmental

Although most stages are of the three basic types just described, we sometimes create special environments for specific productions, some of which may entirely eliminate the separation of stage and audience. In recent years there has been renewed interest in moving out of the theater altogether, as many American theater groups did in the 1960s and 1970s, using real spaces, such as homes, gymnasiums, meeting halls, armories, pools, and even beaches as performance sites. In such cases the proximity of the audience, which may even be interspersed within the performing area, demands total commitment and attention to detail. In fact, in this sort of extremely close situation we sometimes say that we need "no acting at all," but rather a performance that is close to the scale and completeness of everyday life behavior, in the same way that the camera demands full reality in film acting.[1]

Whatever adjustment in scale is required by the space in which you will perform, you know by now that you must justify it by adjusting the level of energy driving your inner process so that the external form of your performance is congruent with the internal form. Whether the space is large and requires larger actions of body and voice, or if it is confined and demands filmlike detail, trust that the audience will willingly join with you in accepting the adjustments required by the conditions of performance.

> EXERCISE 11.1   **JUSTIFYING ADJUSTMENTS IN SCALE**
>
> Use your scene for this experiment in making an adjustment in scale. As you work through your scene, have someone call out one of the types of spaces listed, and immediately adjust and justify the performance as it would be in that space:
>
> 1. BIG: Do the scene as if for a huge proscenium auditorium.
> 2. MEDIUM: Do the scene as if for a moderate-sized thrust stage.
> 3. SMALL: Do the scene as if for a small-arena stage or a film.

Directions on Stage

When we discuss movement and position on stage, we use a standard nomenclature that you must learn. Movements toward or away from the audience are described by very old terms that were developed for the proscenium stage at a time when the stage floor was sloped upward away from the audience in order to enhance the illusion of perspective, so today we still say that moving away from the audience is going **upstage**, and moving toward the audience is going **downstage**. To stand "level" with another actor is for both of you to stand at the same distance from the audience. (Moving upstage during a scene so that the other actors are forced to turn their backs on the audience in order to speak to you is called **upstaging**. This is a cardinal sin and will justifiably cause real condemnation from your fellow actors; avoid it.)

Lateral directions are described from the actors' point of view as they face the audience. Thus, **stage right** is the same as the audience's left; "downstage right" means toward the audience and to the actor's right (see Figure 11.2).

---

[1]The demands of film acting are described in detail in Robert Benedetti, ACTION! Acting for Film and Television (Boston: Allyn & Bacon, 2001).

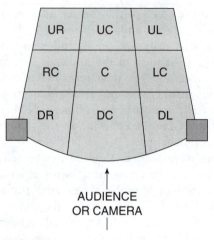

FIGURE 11.2
Locations on a Proscenium Stage

Turns are described as being either **in** (toward the center of the stage, from whichever side of the stage you are on) or **out** (away from the center). **Crossing** (i.e., moving from one point to another) may be in a straight line, or in a slight arc so that you end facing more in profile to the audience. A cross with an exaggerated arc is called a "circle cross" (or sometimes a "banana").

Positions as you pivot relative to the audience are called "one-quarter," "half," and "three-quarters," depending on how far you turn from one side to the other. Thus, a director may tell you to "cheat out one-quarter," which means to pivot 45 degrees away from center. This system of directions can soon become second nature to you.

EXERCISE 11.2   **DIRECTIONS ON STAGE**

Have your partner stand in the center of the stage, with you standing beside him or her on the stage right side. Let your partner "play director" first by giving you the following directions. When you have finished, switch places.

Go down right. / Turn out and go up right. / Take a long cross down left, going upstage of me. / Turn in and do a circle cross up, passing on the downstage side of me and ending level with me on the right. / Cheat out one-quarter. / Circle up to the right around me, and exit left center.

The Groundplan and Blocking

The spatial configuration of the set and the placement of entranceways and furniture or other objects is called the *groundplan*. When the groundplan has been correctly established in a realistic play, the room itself will provide the reason for moving here or there; even in nonrealistic plays and more stylized sets, the spatial logic of the groundplan will encourage you to move in certain ways. As a result, some directors say that "the groundplan really blocks the show."

The patterned use of space within the groundplan is called "blocking." Good stage blocking must reflect the nature of the characters, the character relationships, and most of all the underlying action of the scene. Although the sense of spatial relationship is artistically heightened on the stage, it is based on the way people relate to one another spatially in everyday life. Look around you and observe how the positions people take in a room reflect their relationships and attitudes. Notice also how changes in relationship are reflected by the movements people make, as they move closer or farther away from one another or change position within the space they share. In the same way, good stage blocking always springs from the relationship of the characters and the underlying action of the scene. Blocking at its best expresses things such as "Who is dominant at this moment in the scene? What space does this person control? Who is on whose side? Who is on the attack? Who is retreating? Is there a counterattack?"

Blocking should also reflect the structure of the scene; since a beat change usually signals a shift in the action and a change in the relationship between the characters, it will probably also generate a change in the blocking at that moment. All these are the kinds of impulses you will feel as you experience your action on stage and they are the basis of your blocking. Let yourself move!

When you are working with a director, he or she may have various approaches to blocking. Some directors preplan the blocking in detail and give it to the actors at some point in the rehearsal process; others prefer that the actors provide the impulses that generate the blocking, which the director will then edit as needed.

Regardless of what method your director uses, your main responsibility is to justify your stage movement. Blocking is "dead" movement until you justify it as a believable action performed by your character out of a real need. As a bonus, justified blocking (and dialogue) is easier to remember because it has become a natural expression of your character's action.

If your director requests a piece of blocking that feels awkward, you may have to supply the justification in your own mind. Sometimes a director may be using the blocking to tell you something about the action. If he or she asks you to "move into her," the director may really be saying, "This is where you counterattack."

Because you don't have a director or designer to provide a groundplan for your scene, you and your partner will have to determine it for yourselves. Keep it simple, with the minimum of furniture or props required by the action. You have probably already found the basics of the blocking for your scene during your earlier rehearsals as you felt the impulse to move in relationship to your partner. Build on what you have already discovered, and edit it for clarity and accessibility to the audience, but do not embellish or add movement just for its own sake. For now, don't be overly concerned with onlookers; play directly to one another as if you were on an arena stage, and don't falsify your relationship by cheating out toward the audience.

EXERCISE 11.3 **BLOCKING**

1. Spend a few days watching the "blocking" of everyday life; notice how attitude, relationship, and action are expressed in the way people place themselves in a room and move in relationship to each other.
2. After creating a simple groundplan, lay it out using substitute furniture and work with your partner to block your scene; make the blocking an effective expression of the relationship and action in the scene. Follow your impulses.

Establishing the Score

All the work you have done prior to staging has, in a sense, been dedicated to developing the *content* of the performance. Once the scene begins to live in the performance space and you enter the final stages of rehearsals leading toward the technical and dress rehearsals, you will begin to perfect the *form* of the performance. As the blocking, staging, and other elements of the physical production are being established, you establish a firm and repeatable structure for the inner life of the performance that underlies and motivates the outer form. You do this by setting the sequence of your actions and their objectives, and feeling the logic of that sequence as you move from one objective and action to another. This is what Stanislavski called establishing the **score** of the role. The score is the "map" of your performance, and you will follow it each time you take the journey. The score eventually becomes habitual.

This is the point at which your actor's awareness begins to give way more and more to the character's consciousness; once the score has become completely automatic, then you can give yourself fully to each moment with complete attention to "the here and now," confident in the knowledge that the scene will move toward its proper conclusion. In a way, you must be able to do the scene "in your sleep" in order to be able to do it fully awake.

Stanislavski describes the operation of the score like this:

> With time and frequent repetition, in rehearsal and performance, this score becomes habitual. An actor becomes so accustomed to all his objectives and their sequence that he cannot conceive of approaching his role otherwise than along the line of the steps fixed in the score. Habit plays a great part in creativeness: it establishes in a firm way the accomplishments of creativeness... it makes what is difficult habitual, what is habitual easy, and what is easy beautiful. Habit creates second nature, which is second reality. The score automatically stirs the actor to physical action.[2]

At what point do you commit to a choice and allow a particular element of the score to become habitual? Some actors wait a long time before making their

---

[2]Constantin Stanislavski, *Building a Character*, trans. Elizabeth Reynolds Hapgood (New York: Theatre Arts Books, 1949), p. 70. Theatre Arts Book, 153 Waverly Place, New York, NY 10014.

final choices and approach their roles warily in early rehearsals, gradually filling in the full performance. Others work at performance levels right off, though they maintain enough flexibility to make changes as necessary. You will have to determine your own best approach in relation to the disposition of the director, your fellow actors, the nature of the play, and the length of the rehearsal period. Remember, however, that although you should not make final choices too soon, neither should you lie back and play the waiting game too long; that is unfair to your coworkers since they depend upon you for their reactions even in early rehearsals.

Shaping and Pacing the Performance

When you and your fellow actors have established the score and set the blocking, you begin to experience the shape and flow of the final performance. This shape is now to be perfected as you set what Stanislavski called the *temporhythms* of the performance. Each beat change, each scene crisis, and the momentum toward the major crisis of the play are brought into sharp focus, and the flow of action that connects these milestones is established and smoothed to provide momentum, a sense of drive, urgency, significance, and rising dramatic tension that we call good *pace*; by contrast, a performance lacking in pace feels "flat" and fails to compel our attention. Note that "pace" refers to the *momentum* of the action, whereas the term "**tempo**" refers to its *speed*. A scene may have good pace even when its tempo is very slow as long as the give-and-take between the characters is strong; on the other hand, a fast scene can have poor pace if the connections that drive it are incomplete.

When a performance lacks pace, there is a temptation to speed up or artificially "hype" the action; this is always a mistake. Good pace results only from the natural flow of the action when each transaction of reaction and action between the characters is real and complete. Rushing or forcing the scene only blurs these connections and harms the pace. Paradoxically, poor pace is usually best corrected by taking the time to reestablish the connections within the scene.

The best source of pace is the underlying conflict of the play itself as it lives in each scene. Whatever form the conflict has been given, it provides momentum by driving the conflicting forces that underlie the play against one another as the need for a resolution grows. If you can experience the conflict in this way, scene by scene, it can provide momentum as part of the intrinsic reality of the play, thus avoiding an artificial heightening of energy by rushing or forcing your action.

The given circumstances may also supply good pace by giving the action a sense of urgency: there may be an external deadline that requires that an objective be achieved as quickly as possible, such as someone about to enter, or the fear of discovery. More commonly there is an internal deadline, such as the need to do something before you lose your nerve, to say something before breaking into tears, and so on. Sometimes you can invent circumstances to enhance urgency. The work you did earlier in raising the stakes will serve you well now.

One important element of good pace is *cueing*, the way in which one character begins to speak after another has finished. In real life, if you and I are discussing something, I listen to you in order to understand the idea you are trying to express. When I have grasped that idea, I begin to form my response and am usually ready to begin answering before you have actually finished speaking. Listen to real-life conversations; do you hear how we are often ready to respond even before the other person has stopped talking, and sometimes actually overlap one another's speeches slightly? This way of conversing will produce good cueing on stage.

On the other hand, however, avoid the mistake that some people make in real life of jumping into the other person's statement before they are completely finished. In acting, we call this "stepping on" one another's lines. Good cueing will happen naturally if you will genuinely listen to one another as if you have never heard the dialogue before; the overlap is very slight if it exists at all.

Sometimes pace is harmed by the actors doing "too much," engaging in extraneous business, unnecessary pauses for thought, or emotional displays. Any activity or piece of business that impedes the pace of the scene should be discarded. As Stanislavski was fond of saying, "cut 80 percent." Remember that activity "spends" energy and that you must invest your stage energy with great discrimination; it is often true that "less is more," if it is the right "less."

EXERCISE 11.4   CUEING

Rehearse your scene with your partner to develop the give-and-take of the dialogue so as to establish good cueing, neither stepping on one another's lines nor failing to keep the dialogue flowing in a natural and believable manner.

Costumes, Makeup, and Props

Your preparation for a role is incomplete until you have dealt with your external appearance as determined by costume and makeup. In the Kabuki Theater of Japan, there is a full-length mirror beside the doorway that enters onto the stage. Here, before going on, the Kabuki actor meditates on his external appearance in order to derive from it a sense of the spiritual essence it expresses, and to awaken that spiritual essence in himself—a wonderful example of total justification of the internal and external aspects of the performance. Stanislavski himself would likewise rehearse in full costume and makeup before a mirror before considering his preparation complete.

In a normal rehearsal process, you will have been using substitute props for some time, as well as substitute costume pieces for any items of clothing that affect your movement or business, such as large skirts, robes, or any clothing that is involved in stage business. This is a special concern in period plays in which the clothing may make demands that are considerably different from your everyday reality, and yet you must "live" in those clothes as if they were in fact your everyday garb. Whether the play is period or contemporary, however, it is a good idea for you to get substitute costume and props pieces early on since you must become as familiar with them as your character would be; you may also discover "business" with them that will serve as an effective expression of your action. It is also wise to wear the kind of footwear for rehearsals that will give you the relationship to gravity and posture that is appropriate for your character.

Makeup is too complex a subject to be considered here, and in any case you will not be concerned with it in your scene. Suffice to say that makeup is a study unto itself, and except for the most ordinary "feature heightening" makeup, most actors depend on trained makeup artists to create extensive makeup designs and then to apply them, or to instruct the actor in their application.

During rehearsals you have an important responsibility to treat costume and prop substitutes, and the real items once you have them, with respect. Make sure you have what you need before each rehearsal starts, and return the items in good order after each rehearsal ends. Never leave your props and costumes pieces lying about; remember the old adage, "by his or her tools you shall know the worker."

Technical Rehearsals

The final week or so of the rehearsal period is devoted to incorporating the physical production elements: makeup, props, costumes, set, lights, and sound. Ideally, this is a time of completion and crystallization of your performance; many actors do not feel that their work comes fully to life until all the physical production elements are in place.

In most American theaters, only the final week or two of rehearsal is devoted to the assimilation of all the completed technical elements. This can be a period of tremendous distraction for you if you have not prepared yourself for it in the earlier stages of rehearsal. There are two main ways in which you can be prepared for this final phase: first, to have a solid score (the sequence of objectives) that helps you to keep your focus on the inner action strong without being distracted by all the new external elements; second, to have used good rehearsal substitutes for props, costumes, and groundplan.

Technical rehearsals, when the lighting and sound are assimilated into the production, are especially demanding on the actor. They can take several forms: the most onerous is the *cue to cue* in which the action is interrupted as the production skips from one light or sound cue to another; this kind of rehearsal can disrupt the carefully crafted temporhythms the actors have developed, and a rock-solid score is necessary to overcome this disruption. Less difficult for the actor are the technical rehearsals in which the show plays fully and only stops when an incorrect cue cannot be corrected "on the fly," though this kind of rehearsal can be very lengthy and exhausting. Most congenial are those situations in which the lights and sound have been worked in gradually in the week or so before the technical period and the technical rehearsal can proceed with only rare interruptions. In even the best of situations, however, technical rehearsals take much more time than ordinary rehearsals, and union rules allow for long calls of as much as 12 hours for this purpose. Your stamina, patience, and preparation will be put the test now as at no other time.

Above all, avoid the temptation to suspend your personal work during this final phase of rehearsal. Many fine performances wither on the vine before opening because the outer form becomes the focus of the actor's attention and the inner phase of action ceases to live and grow. Use the addition of the technical elements as an opportunity to explore further the life of the character within a more complete environment.

During this final period, you will probably have less rehearsal time available to you as the energies of the production are taken up with technical matters. It is important that you continue to work on your own to prepare yourself for the coming of the audience. One way to do this is to *visualize* the performance as it would be under audience conditions, and this you can do on your own. Visualization is an excellent form of private rehearsal; it is most effective when used during periods of relaxation, when your deep muscles will actually participate. Here is an exercise in the technique called **visuo-motor behavior rehearsal (VMBR)**, which was first developed for the 1980 Winter Olympics and is used today with great effectiveness by many athletes.

EXERCISE 11.5   VISUO-MOTOR BEHAVIOR REHEARSAL

1. Using the Phasic Relaxation exercise (Exercise 2.2), put yourself into deep muscle relaxation and restful alertness.
2. Now visualize the night when you are about to open in the play from which your scene comes; the theater is ready, you hear the buzz of the audience in the house, and you are standing in your costume with your fellow actors, ready to take your places.
3. In your mind, go into the set, and take your opening position; feel the stage lights shining on you, smell the makeup, feel your clothing, and see your fellow actors and the set.
4. Let the scene begin; live through it totally, and let your deep muscles respond actively to the experience.

Tests have shown that this form of visualized rehearsal can be just as effective as an actual rehearsal, and sometimes more so.

Dress Rehearsal

At last the rehearsal process culminates in the dress rehearsal. Many theaters today have more than one dress rehearsal and in any true dress rehearsal the show should be done under complete performance conditions minus only the audience or with an invited audience. All technical elements are in place, the calls before the show and curtain time are as they will be on opening night, and the actors may not call for lines nor stop for any reason. The aim is to "wean" the show from the freedom to stop during the rehearsal process, and to experience it as an independent and reliable entity that is ready to face an audience.

EXERCISE 11.6 **DRESS REHEARSAL**

Provide any simple furniture or props you need, and dress appropriately for this final rehearsal. Try not to stop for any reason; develop your confidence in being able to complete the scene no matter what; you will need this confidence when you face your audience for the first time.

Summary of Step 11

In the final phase of work, you will consider what adjustments are necessary to make your performance accessible to your audience. An early consideration is the type of stage on which you will perform: Proscenium, thrust, arena, and environmental stages each make special demands. Also, the size of the house will determine adjustments in the scale of your performance.

In this final phase of rehearsal you will set the blocking, which is the way the characters move in relation to one another within the configuration of the groundplan. Good blocking always springs from the relationships of the characters and the underlying action of the scene. During these rehearsals, you are also setting the shape and pace of the scene by clarifying its structure and practicing good cueing.

The shape of the environment in which the play occurs is the groundplan. When the groundplan has been correctly established, the room itself will provide the reason for moving here or there; some directors say that "the groundplan really blocks the show."

Most directors prefer the actors to provide the basic movement impulses that generate the blocking, with the director then editing the pattern as needed. Even if supplied by the director, blocking is "dead" movement until you justify it as a believable action performed by your character out of a real need. Justified blocking (and dialogue) is easy to remember because it has become a natural expression of your character's action.

During this final phase of rehearsal, you set the sequence of actions that forms what Stanislavski called the score of the role. The score eventually becomes habitual; you must be able to do the scene "in your sleep" in order to be able to do it fully awake.

You are also setting the temporhythms of the performance, and are concerned with establishing good pace. One important element of good pace is cueing, the way one character begins to speak after another has finished.

The last week or so of the rehearsal period is devoted to incorporating the physical production elements: makeup, props, costumes, set, lights, and sound. This can be a period of tremendous distraction for you if you have not prepared yourself for it in the earlier stages of rehearsal, but it can also be a time to experience your performance for the first time within a complete physical reality.

STEP 12

The Performance
and After

LEARNING OBJECTIVES

- Experience how the pressure of performance demands adjustments in the way you approach your work.
- Consider the place of emotion and the necessity of spontaneity in your performance.
- Examine the impact of your own fear of failure and desire for success.
- Experience how the presence of the audience ushers in a whole new phase of growth.
- Reflect on your own sense of purpose as an actor and your capacity for transformation.

At last you are ready to put your work before an audience. This is an exciting and, for most of us, an anxious time. As public performance approaches, it helps reduce anxiety to remember that performance is merely one step in the process of creating a show, not an end unto itself. As thorough as your work may have been so far, it is incomplete until you have received and assimilated the contribution of the audience. Go forward to the performance with a spirit of curiosity and eagerness; you don't really know what is in the play or the role until you have shared it with an audience, for it was written to live in the communal moment, and we can never fully anticipate or substitute in rehearsal for the audience's presence. In fact, you will very likely experience your work anew when it is performed, and you may be surprised at how different it may seem.

Emotion in Performance

Young actors sometimes think they must re-create the character's emotion in order to generate each performance "truthfully," but this is an exhausting and unreliable way of working. We may sometimes be tempted to admire the emotionality of an actor who loses control and is overwhelmed by emotion in performance, but a display of emotion for its own sake is never our true purpose. A great actor aspires to use emotional technique to realize the truth of a character according to the demands of the material. Stanislavski said it this way:

> Our art…requires that an actor experience the agony of his role, and weep his heart out at home or in rehearsals, that he then calm himself, get rid of every sentiment alien or obstructive to his part. He then comes out on the stage to convey to the audience in clear, pregnant, deeply felt, intelligible and eloquent terms what he has been through. At this point the spectators will be more affected than the actor, and he will conserve all his forces in order to direct them where he needs them most of all—in reproducing the inner life of the character he is portraying.[1]

The important idea here is that in performance "the spectators will be more affected than the actor." This is necessary for several reasons. First, strong emotion will interfere with an actor's craftsmanship; as Stanislavski put it, "A person in the midst of experiencing a poignant emotional drama is incapable of speaking of it coherently."[2] Second, emotions are unreliable in generating a performance that must be done repeatedly and on schedule. Think of an opera singer who, at the moment the music requires a certain note with a certain feeling, cannot say to the conductor, "I'm not feeling it yet, give me four more measures." This is why Stanislavski once brought a trapeze artist into his training program to help the students experience how, when the moment comes, you must put aside all your fears and ambivalence, and simply jump.

Spontaneity

Everything you do in every performance should feel spontaneous, "as if for the first time," as Aristotle put it, no matter how many times you have done it before. To achieve this spontaneity, you must keep your awareness on your objective, rather than on the mechanics of your external action, just as a baseball batter must think only about the ball and not about his swing. Otherwise you will only be going through the motions, repeating the external aspects of your performance without reexperiencing the internal needs that drive the externals.

Notice that spontaneity does not mean that your performance is erratic or wildly changeable: During the rehearsal process, you gradually refine your external action until it becomes dependable, consistent, stageworthy, and automatic, just as the baseball batter has rehearsed all the aspects of his swing until he can do it without thinking. As Stanislavski said,

---

[1]Constantin Stanislavski, *Building a Character*, trans. Elizabeth Reynolds Hapgood (New York: Theater Arts Books, 1949), p. 70. Theater Arts Books, 153 Waverly Place, New York, NY 10014.

[2]Ibid.

A spontaneous action is one that, through frequent repetition in rehearsal and performance, has become automatic and therefore free.[3]

Because you are able to perform your action without thinking about it, your mind is free to concentrate fully on your objective and to experience your action as if for the first time and in the here and now. This is the freedom that your work in establishing the score has given you: You have internalized your performance as deeply as the baseball batter has internalized his or her swing, as deeply as the dancer has "hard-wired" the choreography into his or her body, and as thoroughly as the pianist has absorbed the score, freeing him or her to "play the music, not the notes."

Beginning the Performance

As you approach your first entrance, you use whatever technique best serves you to reduce and balance muscular tension: You shake out, breathe deeply, do a quick phasic relaxation, stretch, meditate, do a quick VMBR, whatever works best to relax your muscles and clear your mind. Some actors then like to review their beginning objectives, the given circumstances, their relationship to the other character, some key physical quality, perhaps execute the psychological gesture if they have one, or simply to go over the first lines—whatever helps them to enter into the life of the character.

It can be especially useful to re-create your sense of whatever the character has just done or where they have been just before entering; as the old saying has it, *every entrance is an exit from somewhere else.* Being in action as you enter can greatly reduce your anxiety, focus your energy on your objective, and give your entrance compelling vitality and help you to enter into the flow of the scene without disruption.

Underlying your attitude as the performance begins is your curiosity to discover how the performance will live this time; if you can experience it with sufficient awareness and presence you will discover that it is never the same twice, and this provides an endless thrill of discovery and continued artistic growth.

Once you are on, you begin to pursue your objectives and allow the score you have developed to begin to carry you forward. As you get connected to the reality of the scene, you will find that your earlier anxiety dissipates. As one professional football quarterback put it, the best antidote to pregame anxiety is that first good hit.

EXERCISE 12.1   **FINAL PERFORMANCE**

Using substitute furniture, props, and costumes, prepare as complete a final performance of your scene as you are able. If you are in a class situation, consider presenting a program of all the group's final scenes for an invited audience. Allow yourself to be spontaneous, and let emotion arise of its own accord. Experience something of the thrill of an opening night.

---

[3]Constantin Stanislavski, *An Actor's Handbook*, trans. and ed. Elizabeth Reynolds Hapgood (New York: Theater Arts Books, 1936), p. 138. Copyright © 1936, 1961, 1963 by Elizabeth Reynolds Hapgood.

The Fear of Failure

After the performance there will be the inevitable process of evaluation. Did it go well? Did they like it? Was the meaning and reality clear? How can it be improved?

Evaluation is not easy for the actor. If the performance was alive and real, you will find that your memory of it may be fuzzy since you were so engrossed in your action that there was little of your actor awareness available to record what was happening. You will be torn between your own sense of it and your natural interest in the reaction of others, especially when there is disparity between them. Despite the fact that some actors insist that they "never read the reviews," all of us are concerned with evaluation because accurate evaluation is essential to our continued artistic development.

Such objective evaluation and analysis of the performance is, however, inevitably colored by our desire to be accepted and admired, by our fear of failure and its flip side, our desire for success. Everyone has both, of course, though one may be said to be dominant over the other in many individuals. Each is a powerful source of energy, but the differences between them are important: the fear of failure encourages safe and conservative choices, while the desire for success can inspire us to take creative risks.

At the 1984 Olympics in Los Angeles, for example, the athletes who had won medals were tested to determine who among them were driven primarily by a desire for success and who were motivated primarily by the fear of failure. It was found that over 70 percent of these medalists were driven by the desire for success, while less than 30 percent were motivated by the fear of failure. In general, those motivated by fear of failure tended to be technically precise but cautious, while the larger group motivated by desire for success included more "inspired" athletes who were greater risk takers.

No one has ever tested a group of actors in this way, but I suspect that a larger proportion of actors would be found to be driven by the fear of failure. There are many unsuccessful or marginal actors who hang on in the business for year after undistinguished year, whose work is competent but uninspired, who deliver reliable but cautious performances, and who simply don't "go for it." Their motto seems to be, "nothing ventured, nothing lost."

For one thing, the fear of failure encourages the attitude that "I must do it exactly right," producing, at best, technical skill, precision and consistency. These are qualities that are rewarded for their own sake, but technical skill never entirely compensates for a lack of creative courage. An excessive fear of failure can cause you to censor creative impulses, fearing that "I'll look foolish." When you censor an impulse, you must literally "hold it in," and this causes muscular tension. It is no accident that we tell overly cautious people to "loosen up."

Finally, and most important, the fear of failure may cause you to continually judge your own performance to see if you are "doing it right," and this encourages self-consciousness. As the great American actor George C. Scott once observed in an interview:

> I think you have to be schizoid three different ways to be an actor. You've got to be three different people: you have to be a human being, then you have to be the character you're playing, and on top of that, you've got to be the guy

sitting out there in row 10, watching yourself and judging yourself. That's why most of us are crazy to start with or go nuts once we get into it. I mean, don't you think it's a pretty spooky way to earn a living?

EXERCISE 12.2 THE FEAR OF FAILURE

Think back to your performance: Do you remember censoring yourself? Were you sending yourself messages like, "this isn't working?" Where you holding back from full commitment and awareness? What physical tensions resulted from "holding in" your impulses?

Next time you work, notice these moments of self-censorship as they occur: Simply release the tension, take a breath, and get back to work.

Measuring Success

A working actor needs the drive, courage, and long-term tenacity that a strong desire for success can provide. Each of us must define success for ourselves: What constitutes true success for you?

There are really two ways of measuring success: In purely internal terms like pride, sense of accomplishment, feelings of growth; and by external measurements like reviews, grades, and the response of the audience. Obviously, all actors are, and should be, concerned with both. What we need is perspective and balance between the two.

Most actors err on the side of emphasizing external measures of success over internal ones. Even if they have a sense of their own work, they usually don't trust it completely, and they feel so dependent on the opinions of others that a negative response from anyone damages their self-esteem.

Of course, it hurts any actor when their work is not received well. But the serious actor strives to balance the healthy desire for immediate success with the equally important long-range demands of artistic development. You should approach each new role, each rehearsal, and each performance with a desire not only to please others but also to learn and grow for yourself. When evaluating the experience, you must not only ask "Did I do the job well" but also "Am I now a better actor for having done it?"

Winning parts, applause, and good reviews, as important as these things are, are not enough. I know some actors, especially in film and television, who are wildly successful in commercial terms but who derive little personal satisfaction from their careers. The "business" demands that they use the same skills, play the same sort of character in the same type of material, role after role. No matter how highly developed these skills may become, they can bring only limited artistic satisfaction.

Serious actors insist on continuing to develop and extend their abilities with disciplined regularity throughout their lifetime. There is no real substitute for meeting the day-to-day demands of rehearsal and performance; this is why the actor in a repertory company, preparing a continual variety of roles, may develop much faster than the actor who works in long runs, or repeatedly plays the same kinds of roles.

EXERCISE 12.3 **MEASURING SUCCESS**

Think back to your performance; did you have your own independent evaluation of it? Did you trust that evaluation? How did the comments of others affect you? Did you distinguish between the short-term measurement of your success in the role and the long-term benefits of the work to you as a developing artist?

Growth After Opening

Although as a student you will have little chance to experience multiple performances over any significant period of time, you should be aware that in the live theater the opening of a show is never the completion of an actor's work, but only the start of a new phase of the growth process.

The audience contributes to the performance in many ways, perhaps most by providing the responses that complete the rhythmic shaping of the work. These responses take many forms, from the overt (such as laughter or sobs) to the covert (such as rapt stillness or restlessness, or just the "feeling" inside the auditorium). Whatever their form, the audience's responses are an important element in the rhythm of a scene and an experienced writer may well have anticipated them (as least unconsciously) and made provision for them in the rhythms of the material.

So far, you have been guessing what those responses would be—and if you had a director, he or she would have been substituting for them as "an ideal audience of one"—but now that your show has opened you have the real thing and you can fine-tune the shape and flow of your performance accordingly. This is the business of preview performances, or invited audiences at dress rehearsals; in the profession these early exposures to audiences were once the purpose of out-of-town tryouts, though this practice has become economically difficult. It is during these initial exposures to an audience that much is learned which may result in reshaping, even rewriting, or other adjustments to the show. Even a great play like *The Glass Menagerie* underwent a crucial process of development during its first performances in Chicago when a discerning critic fought to keep it alive despite an initially disappointing reception.

The audience's presence will also cause a change in the way you experience your own work; some things you thought would work well may turn out to be too personal or obscure, while other things that you hadn't really noticed may turn out to be powerful or worth developing further. At last you have a sure basis for judgment.

These early experiences with an audience will naturally cause you to begin economizing. You will find after a time that you expended more energy during rehearsals than you do in performance and that you will generally expend less and less energy as the run continues. This is not because you begin doing your part mechanically, but because you are penetrating deeper and deeper to its essence; as this happens, nonessential detail begins to fall away. Your performance is made more effective by distilling it to its essentials in this way; you are doing more with less.

Sadly, in our commercial theater the growth and development of a show may be restricted after opening by the idea that the show is now a commodity that must be delivered unchanged to each subsequent audience. In a professional production, the stage manager is charged with maintaining the show in the condition it was left by the director; the stage manager is in charge even of replacing actors when necessary by drilling their replacements in the performance as established by their predecessors, as if it were possible to change actors the way one might change spark plugs in a car. In some European countries, famous productions are sometimes revived years later with careful attention to the details set down in the original prompt books, like a kind of theatrical taxidermy.

Nevertheless, enlightened theater makers, especially those who have their own companies, view a show as an ongoing creative entity that will continue to develop, like any living thing. As American director Alan Schneider once observed, shows are never finished, only abandoned.

Your Sense of Purpose

When actors want to pay another actor a real compliment, they say they're "a real pro." But what is it that defines a professional? In athletics, we distinguish between professional and amateur on the basis of money: The professional is paid, while the amateur (from the root amat, "to love") participates only for the love of the sport itself. But in acting, "professional" means much more than whether someone is paid; the term carries an implication of integrity, reliability, high standards, and most of all commitment to an ethical standard.

The root of the word comes from an old French verb, *profes*, that meant "to make a solemn vow," as in joining a religious order. In our culture, professionals of all kinds have special knowledge or skills that give them power over other people: Doctors, lawyers, clergymen, and others of the "professional class" are responsible for the well-being of those they serve. Society has placed a special trust in them, and in return they are expected to use their special powers only for the benefit of others. Thus, a professional is someone who has taken a solemn vow (has *professed*) an *ethical standard to use their talent for good*. They have accepted personal responsibility for work that will affect the lives of others. We don't usually take acting as seriously as that, but it is true that at its best, the work of the actor can change people's lives and perhaps even change society. With this power comes a public responsibility for the well-being of those whose lives you will affect, and this demands an enormous commitment.

This commitment operates on three levels simultaneously: First, you must be committed to your own development as an artist; second, to your work; and third, to the world you serve through your work. Acceptance of this social responsibility gives you a sense of purpose to something greater than yourself, and this can give you courage and lead you to extraordinary accomplishments. Theater is the most human of all the arts, and we can preserve and expand our humanity through our art in ways denied us by everyday life. As American playwright David Mamet says,

Who is going to speak up? Who is going to speak for the American spirit? For the human spirit?

Who is capable of being heard? Of being accepted? Of being believed? Only that person who speaks without ulterior motives, without hope of gain, without even the desire to change, with only the desire to create: The artist. The actor. The strong, trained actor dedicated to the idea that the theater is the place we go to hear the truth, and equipped with the technical capacity to speak simply and clearly.[4]

Mamet's comment harkens back to the original impulses of the founders of our modern school of acting when, more than a century ago, Stanislavski and his partner Nemirovich-Danchenko debated the requirements for actors to be taken into their new company at the Moscow Art Theater:

"Take actor A," we would test each other. "Do you consider him talented?"
"To a high degree."
"Will you take him into the troupe?"
"No."
"Why?"
"Because he has adapted himself to his career, his talents to the demands of the
    public, his character to the caprices of the manager, and all of himself to
    theatrical cheapness. A man who is so poisoned cannot be cured."
"And what do you say about Actress B?"
"She is a good actress, but not for us."
"Why?"
"She does not love art, but herself in art."
"And actress C?"
"She won't do. She is incurably given to hokum."
"What about actor D?"
"We should bear him in mind."
"Why?"
"He has ideals for which he is fighting. He is not at peace with present condi-
    tions. He is a man of ideas."
"I am of the same opinion. With your permission I shall enter his name in the
    list of candidates."[5]

It is important for you to consider how you may serve your world through acting. In Step 1 of this book, you wrote a manifesto (Exercise 1.3). Now, at the end of your study, write a new manifesto that reflects what you have learned and what your dreams are now for your own future as an actor and for the American theater itself. Remember that a manifesto is a brief, passionate, and personal statement of belief and purpose. It requires considerable thought, and should be as simple and direct as possible.

---

[4]David Mamet, Writing in Restaurants (New York: Viking Penguin, 1986), p. 21. Copyright © 1986 by David Mamet. All rights reserved.

[5]Constantin Stanislavski, My Life in Art, trans. J. J. Robbins (New York: Theater Arts Books, 1952), pp. 217–218.

EXERCISE 12.4   **YOUR MANIFESTO REDUX**

Make your manifesto just two paragraphs long:

1. What you want to do for the world through your acting: how do you want to make a difference?
2. What techniques and process are necessary to achieve your purpose? What skills and capabilities must you develop to empower yourself to achieve your purpose?
3. When you are satisfied with it, read it aloud in class with full conviction or publish it in some other way.

Transformation

Your sense of purpose grows from your respect for your own talent, your love for the specific material you are performing, and your desire to use both to serve your audience. It is this drive to be at service through your art that will finally overcome the self-consciousness of your ego and carry you beyond yourself, giving you a transcendent purpose from which come dignity, fulfillment, and ongoing artistic vitality.

Stanislavsky called this ongoing artistic vitality "theatrical youthfulness." When we began our study in Step 1, we quoted a portion of remarks he made near the end of his life to a group of young actors who were graduating from The Moscow Art Theater training program. It is appropriate now, at the end of our study, to listen to more of that speech:

> The first essential to retain a youthful performance is to keep the idea of the play alive. That is why the dramatist wrote it and that is why you decided to produce it. One should not be on the stage, one should not put on a play for the sake of acting or producing only. Yes, you must be excited about your profession. You must love it devotedly and passionately, but not for itself, not for its laurels, not for the pleasure and delight it brings to you as artists. You must love your chosen profession because it gives you the opportunity to communicate ideas that are important and necessary to your audience. Because it gives you the opportunity, through the ideas that you dramatize on the stage and through your characterizations, to educate your audience and to make them better, finer, wiser, and more useful members of society....
>
> You must keep the idea alive and be inspired by it at each performance. This is the only way to retain youthfulness in performance and your own youthfulness as actors. The true recreation of the play's idea—I emphasize the word true—demands from the artist wide and varied knowledge, constant self-discipline, the subordination of his personal tastes and habits to the demands of the idea, and sometimes even definite sacrifices.[6]

The art of acting has always had a very special service to render, one that has become increasingly important today: it is rooted in the actor's ability to

---

[6]Quoted by Nikolai Gorchakov in *Stanislavski Directs* (New York, Funk & Wagnalls, 1954), pp. 40–41.

transform, to become "someone else." At a time when mass culture, big business, and bigger government make us, as individuals, feel more and more insignificant and impotent, the actor's ability to be "in charge" of personal reality can be a source of hope and inspiration to others.

The actor's ability to undergo transformation is itself a kind of potency, a kind of power over the future. While a play may teach us something about who we are, it is the actor's ability to be transformed that teaches us something about whom we may become. The actor's ability to redefine personal reality before our very eyes reminds us of our own spiritual capacity for self-definition, and thus the theater becomes a celebration of our vitality and of the ongoing flow of life.

The actor who works in this spirit finds his or her horizons being continually broadened by a renewed sense of ethical and spiritual purpose. It can be a wonderful time to be an actor.

Summary of Step 12

Once you are finally before an audience, you strive to keep each performance fresh and spontaneous without making it erratic. Your emotional experience should be controlled and should not become an end in itself.

You should evaluate your work not only in terms of the response of others but also in terms of your own long-term growth objectives. The opening of a show is never the completion of your work, but only the start of a new phase of the growth process. At last you will have a sure basis for judgment, and you will penetrate deeper and deeper to the essence of your role; as this happens, nonessential detail begins to fall away. Your performance is made more effective by distilling it to its essentials; you will be doing more with less.

As an actor, your sense of purpose and your commitment to serve your world through your work will give you courage and ongoing artistic vitality.

APPENDIX A

The Tradition of the Actor

LEARNING OBJECTIVES

- Outline and appreciate a condensed history of Western acting with special emphasis on the modern period and its precursors in ancient times.

Today's actor belongs to a long tradition, and having a sense of belonging to this tradition can inform your work and be a great source of energy and courage.

Our Western acting tradition began in ancient Greece when towns would send male choric groups to compete against one another in the recitation of poems at religious festivals held in honor of Dionysus, the god of wine, transformation, and the life force itself. Gradually, the chorus leader began to speak as an individual character, and many historians consider this chorus leader to be the prototype of the actor.

Eventually, two other actors were added, thus creating dialogue, and so plays as we know them were born. In 534 BCE, a contest for tragedy was established in Athens and was won by the first known actor, Thespis; the word *thespian* comes from his name. Performing in large outdoor amphitheaters, these early actors wore masks to indicate the characters they played, and each actor appeared in several parts.

Over the next thousand years, the center of our Western theater tradition shifted from Greece to Rome. The Roman actors no longer wore masks, and plays became more spectacular, as well as more violent and licentious. When the Roman Catholic Church rose to power, it outlawed the theater, and around 400 CE actors were excommunicated. They remained outside the graces of the church—and polite society—for more than a thousand years thereafter.

In the Middle Ages, there was no theater in our modern sense, but traveling troubadours visited noble households telling stories in verse and song. These itinerant performers served the important function of carrying local dialects from one region to another, helping to create the national languages of Europe and England as we know them today.

The rebirth of the theater began in the 900s with brief playlets telling biblical stories performed in Latin by priests and choirboys as part of church services. Beginning in the 1200s, religious plays were expanded and moved outdoors; the actors were no longer priests or choirboys but members of nonreligious organizations such as trade guilds, like the rustics portrayed in Shakespeare's *A Midsummer Night's Dream*. Meanwhile, in the universities, plays were being written imitating classical Greek drama and these

140

were produced in small private theaters for the aristocracy, often performed by the courtiers themselves.

The rebirth of the professional actor happened about this time, not in the church or university, but in the banquet hall and courtyard. The nobility began to accompany dinners and other social events with comedic skits and legendary stories acted out by skilled performers. To provide these performances, troupes of actors began to travel from household to household, like the players in Shakespeare's *Hamlet*, performing comical interludes based on folktales. Meanwhile, in Italy, the Commedia dell'Arte featured a traditional cast of characters and improvised dialogue. All these kinds of traveling players performed for nobility but also sometimes in market squares and at public festivals, eking out a living from their craft.

In Elizabethan England, plays developed in the late 1500s when a new group of playwrights merged the interludes performed by wandering actors with the classically inspired plays of the universities. To perform these plays, companies of professional actors were formed under the sponsorship of nobles, and the business of public theater as we know it was born. The actors in these companies received regular salaries, and the leading actors were shareholders who received a portion of the box office income.

Acting continued to develop as a profession throughout the 1600s with the emergence of companies run by strong actor/managers. Up to this time, all female parts had been played by young boys (there were even all-boy companies), but in the 1660s actresses began to appear regularly on the English stage. For many years these actresses were widely regarded as women of loose morals. In fact, up to that time both male and female actors were still denied burial in consecrated ground.

During the 1700s, actors became increasingly important and respectable. Audiences were attracted to star performers rather than to particular plays. In the 1740s, David Garrick brought greater realism to English acting, although the dominant style of acting for the next 150 years would seem artificial by today's standards.

The Twentieth Century

It was not until the turn of the twentieth century, with the work of Constantin Stanislavski (1863–1938) and his Moscow Art Theatre, that the truly modern actor was born, an actor devoted to searching for the truth of human behavior through systematic discipline and to making the world a better place through the ideas and experiences an actor could bring to an audience. Stanislavski's approach soon established itself as the dominant technique from his time to the present day. In its earliest form, Stanislavski's work stressed psychological and emotional techniques that encouraged the actor to work "from the inside out." Later, however, he switched to a more physical approach called the Method of Physical Actions. Throughout his life, Stanislavski continued to change and develop his "system."

Over many years, Stanislavski's method began to spread as his books were translated from the Russian and actors who had worked with him traveled to other countries. In the United States, a number of acting teachers developed their own versions of Stanislavski's work, each emphasizing various features drawn from different stages of its development. Through the work of teachers like Lee Strasberg, Sanford Meisner, Uta Hagen, and others, various forms of the method, some quite different from one other and different even from Stanislavski's work at various stages of its development, became influential in the American theater of the mid-twentieth century. Few of these reflected the entire breadth of Stanislavski's own lifelong search and development, and it is only recently that we are coming to appreciate the whole arc of his work from his early emphasis on internal thought processes to his later experiments in externals in what he called the "method of physical actions."

A contemporary of Stanislavski's, Vsevolod Meyerhold (1874–1940), reacted against Stanislavski's approach and developed another kind of acting that borrowed from Asian theater and the storytelling spirit of the itinerant performer. Where Stanislavski's aim was to represent the truth of behavior through naturalistic means, Meyerhold's theater was presentational and overtly theatrical. Focused not on the psychology of behavior but on the structure of the body, Meyerhold's central discipline was called *biomechanics*. It used physical training to forge the connection between mind and body, to "teach the body to think." It began with simple activities like running and jumping and then progressed to leaps and rolls, movement with objects, movement up and down ramps and stairs, partner lifts, and acrobatics, culminating in highly stylized movement pieces choreographed by Meyerhold himself. Eventually, Meyerhold wanted the actor to achieve a state of total mind–body integration. (The contrast between Stanislavski's psychological approach and Meyerhold's physical approach mirrors the split in the world of psychology occurring at about the same time, between Freud's talk therapy and Wilhelm Reich's psychophysical work.) Meyerhold's physical approach was the fountainhead of an alternative tradition that paralleled Stanislavski's and inspired various avant-garde experiments throughout the twentieth century.

A few years later, a German playwright and director, Bertolt Brecht (1898–1956), borrowed elements of both Stanislavski's and Meyerhold's methods. His theater was, like Meyerhold's, overtly theatrical, but the actors worked to create characters who were as real as those of Stanislavski. The difference was that although the character's behavior was fully rendered, the actor presented it in the spirit of a **demonstration** in order to express a judgment on it. This required the actor to maintain a slight "distance" from the character, in contrast to the absolute identification with a character demanded by Stanislavski. Brecht used his theater to promote social change by making the spectators see everyday behavior in a new light by his "distancing effect" and thereby encouraging them to think about the ramifications of their own behavior and beliefs.

In the mid-twentieth century, the ideas of French actor/director Antonin Artaud (1896–1948) were especially influential in the avant-garde theater, even though Artaud never developed a specific body of technique. His four central concepts were as follows: (a) the actor sacrifices himself or herself in the act of performing; (b) the language of theater is primarily movement and sound rather than words; (c) the actor's movement and sound have their own meanings and penetrate the spectators directly; and (d) the resulting experience can move the spectators to a heightened state of spiritual awareness that forces them to confront their true natures.

The Polish director Jerzy Grotowski (1933–1999) used Artaud's ideas to develop a training program and body of technique based on the idea of the "Holy" actor—that is, an actor who surrenders the self totally in the act of performing. This sacrifice is achieved by rigorous physical and vocal training (called "plastique" exercises) so extreme that they break down all obstacles between impulse and expression and therefore make deception or self-censorship impossible. The authentic soul of the actor in performance becomes visible, and experiencing such a performance can encourage the audience to begin to live in a similar way.

In the social ferment of America in the 1960s and 1970s, the influence of Meyerhold, Brecht, Artaud, and Grotowski inspired many avant-garde theaters, such as the Living Theatre created by Judith Malina and Julian Beck, the Open Theatre created by Joseph Chaikin, and the Performance Group created by Richard Schechner; political theaters, such as the Bread and Puppet Theatre created by Peter Schumann; and the longest-lived American theater, the San Francisco Mime Troupe, originally led by R. G. Davis. Each developed its own approaches to acting, but they all had several things in common. First, like Meyerhold, they were all primarily physical in their approach and stressed body and vocal work in the training of actors as well as extraordinary uses of the body and voice in performance. Second, like Artaud they were all aimed at creating theater experiences that produced powerful spiritual changes in the audience, experiences communicated primarily through physical rather than intellectual means.

As the same time that these radical theater groups were creating an alternative theater movement, the naturalistic tradition of Stanislavski was continuing in the main-stream theater.

The influence of non-Western theater has been important throughout our history and had been part of the philosophies of Stanislavski, Meyerhold, Brecht, and Grotowski; several early visionaries had experimented with it in productions like Orson Welles' "Voodoo Macbeth" in 1936. From the 1960s onward directors like Richard Schechner began to examine non-Western forms in greater detail and to incorporate them directly into our training and performing vocabulary. From Japan we took the influence of the masked Zen-Buddhist Noh theater, the highly stylized Kabuki, and the detailed and complex Bunraku puppet theater; from China came the influence of the acrobatic Peking Opera; from India came the precision of the Kathakali dancers; and from Malaysia and other Arab lands came shadow puppetry.

Some specific examples of the non-Western influence were Brecht's use of Peking Opera techniques in developing his Epic Theatre form; Antonin Artaud's fascination with Balinese dance as a source of his "Theatre of Cruelty"; the influence of Kathakali dance on the style of French director Ariane Mnouchkine and her Théâtre du Soleil; the rigorous physical training of Japanese director Tadashi Suzuki, now used in several American training programs; and most famously, the use of Indonesian puppet theater devices by director Julie Taymor in productions like *The Lion King*.

The evolution of the actor has continued to the present day as serious training programs have assimilated all these and many other influences. This has produced a rich mix of philosophies and techniques in which any actor can find a place for his or her unique energies. It is a wonderful time to be an actor!

APPENDIX B

Suggested Plays and Anthologies

Plays

The following American plays are good sources of scenes with the qualities most useful for the exercises in this book. Most of these plays are available in inexpensive paperback "acting editions" from the publishers indicated.

After the Fall by Arthur Miller (Dramatists Play Service)

Ah, Wilderness! by Eugene O'Neill (Samuel French)

All My Sons by Arthur Miller (Dramatists Play Service)

The Amen Corner by James Baldwin (Samuel French)

American Buffalo by David Mamet (Samuel French)

The Andersonville Trial by Saul Levitt (Dramatists Play Service)

And Miss Reardon Drinks a Little by Paul Zindel (Dramatists Play Service)

Angels in America by Tony Kushner (Theatre Communications Group)

Anna Christie by Eugene O'Neill (Vintage Books)

Art by Yasmina Reza, translated by Christopher Hampton (Dramatists Play Service)

August: Osage County by Tracy Letts (Dramatists Play Service)

Bedrooms: Five Comedies by Renee Taylor and Joseph Bologna (Samuel French)

Bent by Martin Sherman (Samuel French)

Birdbath by Leonard Melfi (Samuel French)

Born Yesterday by Garson Kanin (Dramatists Play Service)

Cat on a Hot Tin Roof by Tennessee Williams (Dramatists Play Service)

Chapter Two by Neil Simon (Samuel French)

The Chase by Horton Foote (Dramatists Play Service)

The Children's Hour by Lillian Hellman (Dramatists Play Service)

Clybourne Park by Bruce Norris (Theatre Communications Group)

The Colored Museum by George C. Wolfe (Broadway Play Publishing)

Come Back, Little Sheba by William Inge (Samuel French)

Come Back to the 5 & Dime, Jimmy Dean, Jimmy Dean by Ed Graczyk (Samuel French)

A Coupla White Chicks Sitting Around Talking by John Ford Noonan (Samuel French)

Crimes of the Heart by Beth Henley (Dramatists Play Service)

Crossing Delancey by Susan Sandler (Samuel French)

The Crucible by Arthur Miller (Dramatists Play Service)

The Dark at the Top of the Stairs by William Inge (Dramatists Play Service)

A Day in the Death of Joe Egg by Peter Nichols (Samuel French)

Death of a Salesman by Arthur Miller (Dramatists Play Service)

The Death of Bessie Smith by Edward Albee (Plume)

A Delicate Balance by Edward Albee (Samuel French)

Division Street by Steve Tesich (Samuel French)

Doubt by John Patrick Shanley (Dramatists Play Service)

Duet for One by Tom Kempinski (Samuel French)

The Eccentricities of a Nightingale by Tennessee Williams (Dramatists Play Service)

Effect of Gamma Rays on Man-in-the-Moon Marigolds by Paul Zindel (Bantam)

Enter Laughing by Joseph Stein (Samuel French)

Euridyce by Sarah Ruhl (Samuel French)

Extremities by William Mastrosimone (Samuel French)

Fences by August Wilson (Samuel French)

Fool for Love by Sam Shepard (Dramatists Play Service)

Frankie and Johnny in the Clair de Lune by Terrence McNally (Dramatists Play Service)

The Gingerbread Lady by Neil Simon (Samuel French)

The Glass Menagerie by Tennessee Williams (Dramatists Play Service)

Glengarry Glen Ross by David Mamet (Samuel French)

Golden Boy by Clifford Odets (Dramatists Play Service)

God of Carnage by Yasmina Reza (Dramatists Play Service)

A Hatful of Rain by Michael Vincente Gazzo (Samuel French)

The Heidi Chronicles by Wendy Wasserstein (Dramatists Play Service)

The House of Blue Leaves by John Guare (Samuel French)

How I Learned to Drive by Paula Vogel (Dramatists Play Service)

The Immigrant by Mark Harelik (Broadway Play Publishing)

I Never Sang for My Father by Robert Anderson (Dramatists Play Service)

I Ought to Be in Pictures by Neil Simon (Samuel French)

Intimate Apparel by Lynn Nottage (Dramatists Play Service)

It Had to Be You by Renee Taylor and Joseph Bologna (Samuel French)

The Laramie Project by Moises Kaufman et al (Dramatists Play Service)

The Last Night of Ballyhoo by Alfred Uhry (Dramatists Play Service)

Last of the Red Hot Lovers by Neil Simon (Samuel French)

Last Summer at Bluefish Cove by Jane Chambers (JH Press)

Laundry and Bourbon by James McLure (Dramatists Play Service)

A Lie of the Mind by Sam Shepard (Dramatists Play Service)

The Little Foxes by Lillian Hellman (Dramatists Play Service)

Long Day's Journey into Night by Eugene O'Neill (Yale University Press)

Look Homeward, Angel by Ketti Frings (Samuel French)

Lost in Yonkers by Neil Simon (Samuel French)

Lovers and Other Strangers by Renee Taylor and Joseph Bologna (Samuel French)

Luv by Murray Schisgal (Dramatists Play Service)

The Matchmaker by Thornton Wilder (Samuel French)

The Middle Ages by A. R. Gurney, Jr. (Dramatists Play Service)

Moonchildren by Michael Weller (Samuel French)

A Moon for the Misbegotten by Eugene O'Neill (Samuel French)

Murder at the Howard Johnson's by Ron Clark and Sam Bobrick (Samuel French)

The Nerd by Larry Shue (Dramatists Play Service)

'Night, Mother by Marsha Norman (Dramatists Play Service)

The Night of the Iguana by Tennessee Williams (Dramatists Play Service)

No Place to Be Somebody by Charles Gordone (Samuel French)

The Odd Couple (Female Version) by Neil Simon (Samuel French)

The Odd Couple (Male Version) by Neil Simon (Samuel French)

Of Mice and Men by John Steinbeck (Dramatists Play Service)

Oh Dad, Poor Dad, Mamma's Hung You in the Closet and I'm Feelin' So Sad by Arthur Kopit (Samuel French)

The Only Game in Town by Frank D. Gilroy (Samuel French)

On the Open Road by Steve Tesich (Samuel French)

Other Desert Cities by Jon Robin Baitz (Grove Press)

The Philadelphia Story by Philip Barry (Samuel French)

The Piano Lesson by August Wilson (Samuel French)

Picnic by William Inge (Dramatists Play Service)

The Prisoner of Second Avenue by Neil Simon (Samuel French)

Proof by David Auburn (Dramatists Play Service)

Rabbit Hole by David Lindsay-Abaire (Dramatists Play Service)

The Rainmaker by N. Richard Nash (Samuel French)

A Raisin in the Sun by Lorraine Hansberry (Samuel French)

Red by John Logan (Dramatists Play Service)

The Red Coat by John Patrick Shanley (Dramatists Play Service)

Ruined by Lynn Nottage (Dramatists Play Service)

Scenes from American Life by A. R. Gurney, Jr. (Samuel French)

The Sea Horse by Edward J. Moore (Samuel French)

Sexual Perversity in Chicago by David Mamet (Samuel French)

The Shadow Box by Michael Cristofer (Samuel French)

The Sign in Sidney Brustein's Window by Lorraine Hansberry (Samuel French)

Six Degrees of Separation by John Guare (Dramatists Play Service)

Speed-the-Plow by David Mamet (Samuel French)

Splendor in the Grass by William Inge (Dramatists Play Service)

Spoils of War by Michael Weller (Samuel French)

Steel Magnolias by Robert Harling (Dramatists Play Service)

Strange Snow by Stephen Metcalfe (Samuel French)

A Streetcar Named Desire by Tennessee Williams (Dramatists Play Service)

The Subject Was Roses by Frank D. Gilroy (Samuel French)

Summer and Smoke by Tennessee Williams (Dramatists Play Service)

Sweet Bird of Youth by Tennessee Williams (Dramatists Play Service)

Sylvia by A. R. Gurney (Dramatists Play Service)

The Tenth Man by Paddy Chayefsky (Samuel French)

That Championship Season by Jason Miller (Samuel French)

The Time of Your Life by William Saroyan (Samuel French)

To Gillian on Her Thirty-Seventh Birthday by Michael Brady (Broadway Play Publishing)

To Kill a Mockingbird by Christopher Sergel from the novel by Harper Lee (Dramatic Publishing)

A Touch of the Poet by Eugene O'Neill (Random House)

Toys in the Attic by Lillian Hellman (Dramatists Play Service)

Tribute by Bernard Slade (Samuel French)

True West by Sam Shepard (Samuel French)

Twice Around the Park by Murray Schisgal (Samuel French)

A View from the Bridge by Arthur Miller (Dramatists Play Service)

Vikings by Stephen Metcalfe (Samuel French)

Waiting for Lefty by Clifford Odets (Grove Press)

What I Did Last Summer by A. R. Gurney, Jr. (Dramatists Play Service)

When You Comin' Back, Red Ryder? by Mark Medoff (Dramatists Play Service)

Wit by Margaret Edson (Dramatists Play Service)

Who's Afraid of Virginia Woolf? by Edward Albee (Dramatists Play Service)

The Women by Clare Boothe Luce (Dramatists Play Service)

Yellowman by Dael Orlandersmith (Vintage)

The Zoo Story by Edward Albee (Dramatists Play Service)

Zoot Suit and Other Plays by Luis Valdez (Arte Publico Press)

Play and Scene Anthologies

A number of anthologies of scenes are available for student actors; they can be found in specialty book stores or online. Most of these books index scenes in a variety of ways (male–male, female–male, female–female, and by genre and ethnicity). They can be useful for picking a scene, but remember that for our purposes you must also read the entire play from which the scene comes.

One-Act Plays for Acting Students: An Anthology of Short One-Act Plays for One, Two, or Three Actors, ed. Norman Bert (Meriwether)

24 Favorite One-Act Plays, ed. Bennett Cerf, Van H. Cartmell (Main Street Books)

99 Film Scenes for Actors, ed. Angela Nicholas (Avon)

The Actor's Book of Scenes from New Plays, ed. Eric Lane (Penguin USA)

The Actor's Scenebook, ed. Michael Schulman (Bantam Books)

The Best American Short Plays 1997–1998, ed. Glenn Young (Applause Theatre Books)

The Best American Short Plays 1999–2000, ed. Glenn Young (Applause Theatre Books)

The Best American Short Plays 2000–2001, ed. Mark Glubke (Applause Theatre Books)

Duo! Best Scenes for the 90's (Applause Acting Series), ed. John Horvath, Byrna Wortman, Lavonne Mueller, Jack Temchin (Applause Theatre Books)

Duo! Best Scenes of the 90's, ed. John Horvath (Applause Theatre Books)

Famous American Plays of the 70's (The Laurel Drama Series), ed. Ted Hoffman (Laurel)

Five Comic One-Act Plays by Anton Chekhov (Dover Thrift Editions)

Great Scenes and Monologues for Actors, ed. Eva Mekler, Michael Schulman (St. Martin's Press)

Great Scenes and Monologues for Actors, ed. Michael Schulman (St. Martin's Press)

In Performance: Contemporary Monologues for Women and Women, Late Teens to Twenties, ed. JV mercanti (Applause Theatre & Cinema Books)

Plays for Young Audiences: An Anthology of Selected Plays for Young Audiences, ed. Max Bush, Roger Ellis (Meriwether)

Plays from the Contemporary American Theatre, ed. Brooks McNamara (Signet)

The Scenebook for Actors, ed. Norman A. Bert (Meriwether)

Scenes and Monologs from the Best New Plays, ed. Roger Ellis (Meriwether)

Scenes and Monologues of Spiritual Experience from the Best Contemporary

Plays, ed. Roger Ellis (Applause Theatre & Cinema Books)

The Ultimate Scene and Monologue Source Book, by Ed Hooks (Backstage Books)

Wordplays 5: An Anthology of New American Drama: Plays by James Strahs, James Lapine–Stephen Sondheim, Des McAnuff, John Jesurun, Kathy Acker (PAJ)

Wordplays: An Anthology of New American Drama by Maria Fornes, Ronald Tavel, Jean-Claude Van Itallie, William Hauptman (Farrar, Straus, and Giroux)

Anthologies for Students of Color

Asian American Drama: 9 Plays from the Multiethnic Landscape, ed. Brian Nelson (Applause Theatre Books)

Beyond the Pale: Dramatic Writing from First Nations Writers & Writers of Color, ed. Yvette Nolan (Consortium Books)

Black Comedy: Nine Plays, ed. Pamela Faith Jackson, Karimah (Applause Theatre Books)

Black Drama in America: An Anthology, ed. Darwin T. Turner (Howard University Press)

Black Theatre USA Revised and Expanded Edition, Vol. 1: Plays by African Americans from 1847 to Today, ed. James V. Hatch, Ted Shine (Free Press)

Black Thunder: An Anthology of Contemporary African American Drama, ed. William B. Branch (Signet)

Colored Contradictions: An Anthology of Contemporary African-American Plays, ed. Robert Alexander, Harry Justin Elam (Plume Books)

Contemporary Plays by Women of Color, ed. Kathy A. Perkins (Routledge)

Drama for a New South Africa: Seven Plays, ed. David Graver (Indiana University Press)

The Fire This Time: African American Plays for the 21st Century, ed. Robert Alexander, Harry Justin Elam (Theatre Communications Group)

Great Scenes from Minority Playwrights: Seventy-Four Scenes of Cultural Diversity, ed. Marsh Cassady (Meriwether)

Latin American Theatre in Translation: An Anthology of Works from Mexico, the Caribbean and the Southern Cone, ed. Charles Philip Thomas, Marco Antonio de la Parra (Xlibris)

Moon Marked and Touched by Sun: Plays by African-American Women, ed. Sydne Mahone (Theatre Communications Group)

Multicultural Theatre II: Contemporary Hispanic, Asian and African-American Plays, ed. Roger Ellis (Meriwether)

The National Black Drama Anthology: Eleven Plays from America's Leading African-American Theaters, ed. Woodie King, Jr. (Applause Theatre Books)

Playwrights of Color, ed. Meg Swanson, Robin Murray (Intercultural Press)

Political Stages: A Dramatic Anthology, ed. Emily Mann, David Roessel (Applause Theatre Books)

Seven Black Plays: The Theodore Ward Prize for African American Playwriting, ed. Chuck Smith (Northwestern)

Seventh Generation: An Anthology of Native American Plays, ed. Mimi D'Aponte (Theatre Communications Group)

Unbroken Thread: An Anthology of Plays by Asian American Women, ed. Roberta Uno (University of Massachusetts Press)

Voices of Color: 50 Scenes and Monologues by African American Playwrights (Applause Acting Series), ed. Woodie King, Jr. (Applause Theatre Books)

War Plays by Women: An International Anthology, ed. Claire M. Tylee, Elaine Turner, Agnes Cardinal (Routledge)

APPENDIX C
Short Practice Selections from Shakespeare

Sonnet 18

Shall I compare thee to a summer's day?

Thou art more lovely and more temperate:

Rough winds do shake the darling buds of May,

And summer's lease hath all too short a date:

Sometime too hot the eye of heaven shines,

And often is his gold complexion dimm'd;

And every fair from fair sometime declines,

By chance or nature's changing course untrimm'd;

But thy eternal summer shall not fade

Nor lose possession of that fair thou owest;

Nor shall Death brag thou wander'st in his shade,

When in eternal lines to time thou growest:

So long as men can breathe or eyes can see,

So long lives this and this gives life to thee.

Sonnet 29

When, in disgrace with fortune and men's eyes,

I all alone beweep my outcast state

And trouble deaf heaven with my bootless cries

And look upon myself and curse my fate,

Wishing me like to one more rich in hope,

Featured like him, like him with friends possess'd,

Desiring this man's art and that man's scope,

With what I most enjoy contented least;

Yet in these thoughts myself almost despising,

Haply I think on thee, and then my state,

Like to the lark at break of day arising

From sullen earth, sings hymns at heaven's gate;

For thy sweet love remember'd such wealth brings

That then I scorn to change my state with kings.

Sonnet 116

Let me not to the marriage of true minds

Admit impediments. Love is not love

Which alters when it alteration finds,

Or bends with the remover to remove:

O no! it is an ever-fixed mark

That looks on tempests and is never shaken;

It is the star to every wandering bark,

Whose worth's unknown, although his height be taken.

Love's not Time's fool, though rosy lips and cheeks

Within his bending sickle's compass come:

Love alters not with his brief hours and weeks,

But bears it out even to the edge of doom.

If this be error and upon me proved,

I never writ, nor no man ever loved.

From *The Comedy of Errors*

Dromio of Ephesus

Return'd so soon! rather approach'd too late:

The capon burns, the pig falls from the spit,

The clock hath strucken twelve upon the bell;

My mistress made it one upon my cheek:

She is so hot because the meat is cold;

The meat is cold because you come not home;

You come not home because you have no stomach;

You have no stomach having broke your fast;

But we that know what 'tis to fast and pray

Are penitent for your default to-day.

Luciana

Why, headstrong liberty is lash'd with woe.

There's nothing situate under heaven's eye

But hath his bound, in earth, in sea, in sky:

The beasts, the fishes, and the winged fowls,

Are their males' subjects and at their controls:

Men, more divine, the masters of all these,

Lords of the wide world and wild watery seas,

Indued with intellectual sense and souls,

Of more preeminence than fish and fowls,

Are masters to their females, and their lords:

Then let your will attend on their accords.

From *Hamlet*

Hamlet

(takes a skull)

Alas, poor Yorick! I knew him, Horatio: a fellow

of infinite jest, of most excellent fancy: he hath

borne me on his back a thousand times; and now, how

abhorred in my imagination it is! my gorge rims at

it. Here hung those lips that I have kissed I know

not how oft. Where be your gibes now? your

gambols? your songs? your flashes of merriment,

that were wont to set the table on a roar? Not one

now, to mock your own grinning? quite chap-fallen?

Now get you to my lady's chamber, and tell her, let

her paint an inch thick, to this favor she must

come; make her laugh at that.

Ophelia

O, what a noble mind is here o'erthrown!

The courtier's, soldier's, scholar's, eye, tongue, sword;

The expectancy and rose of the fair state,

The glass of fashion and the mould of form,

The observed of all observers, quite, quite down!

And I, of ladies most deject and wretched,
That suck'd the honey of his music vows,
Now see that noble and most sovereign reason,
Like sweet bells jangled, out of tune and harsh;
That unmatch'd form and feature of blown youth
Blasted with ecstasy: O, woe is me,
To have seen what I have seen, see what I see!

From *Twelfth Night*
Viola

Make me a willow cabin at your gate,
And call upon my soul within the house;
Write loyal cantons of contemned love
And sing them loud even in the dead of night;
Halloo your name to the reverberate hills
And make the babbling gossip of the air
Cry out 'Olivia!' O, You should not rest
Between the elements of air and earth,
But you should pity me!

From *Taming of the Shrew*
Petruchio

You lie, in faith; for you are call'd plain Kate,
And bonny Kate and sometimes Kate the curst;
But Kate, the prettiest Kate in Christendom
Kate of Kate Hall, my super-dainty Kate,
For dainties are all Kates, and therefore, Kate,
Take this of me, Kate of my consolation;

Hearing thy mildness praised in every town,
Thy virtues spoke of, and thy beauty sounded,
Yet not so deeply as to thee belongs,
Myself am moved to woo thee for my wife.

Katharina

Fie, fie! unknit that threatening unkind brow,
And dart not scornful glances from those eyes,
To wound thy lord, thy king, thy governor:
It blots thy beauty as frosts do bite the meads,
Confounds thy fame as whirlwinds shake fair buds,
And in no sense is meet or amiable.
A woman moved is like a fountain troubled,
Muddy, ill-seeming, thick, bereft of beauty;
And while it is so, none so dry or thirsty
Will deign to sip or touch one drop of it.

From *Romeo and Juliet*
Romeo

But, soft! what light through yonder window breaks?
It is the east, and Juliet is the sun.
Arise, fair sun, and kill the envious moon,
Who is already sick and pale with grief,
That thou her maid art far more fair than she:
Be not her maid, since she is envious;
Her vestal livery is but sick and green

And none but fools do wear it; cast it off.

It is my lady, O, it is my love!

O, that she knew she were!

Juliet

O Romeo, Romeo! wherefore art thou Romeo?

Deny thy father and refuse thy name;

Or, if thou wilt not, be but sworn my love,

And I'll no longer be a Capulet.

'Tis but thy name that is my enemy;

Thou art thyself, though not a Montague.

What's Montague? it is nor hand, nor foot,

Nor arm, nor face, nor any other part

Belonging to a man. O, be some other name!

What's in a name? that which we call a rose

By any other name would smell as sweet;

So Romeo would, were he not Romeo call'd,

Retain that dear perfection which he owes

Without that title. Romeo, doff thy name,

And for that name which is no part of thee

Take all myself.

From *Measure for Measure*

Claudio

Ay, but to die, and go we know not where;

To lie in cold obstruction and to rot;

This sensible warm motion to become

A kneaded clod; and the delighted spirit

To bathe in fiery floods, or to reside

In thrilling region of thick-ribbed ice;

To be imprison'd in the viewless winds,

And blown with restless violence round about

The pendent world; or to be worse than worst

Of those that lawless and incertain thought

Imagine howling: 'tis too horrible!

The weariest and most loathed worldly life

That age, ache, penury and imprisonment

Can lay on nature is a paradise

To what we fear of death.

From *A Midsummer Night's Dream*

Hermia

Puppet? why so? ay, that way goes the game.

Now I perceive that she hath made compare

Between our statures; she hath urged her height;

And with her personage, her tall personage,

Her height, forsooth, she hath prevail'd with him.

And are you grown so high in his esteem;

Because I am so dwarfish and so low?

How low am I, thou painted maypole? speak;

How low am I? I am not yet so low

But that my nails can reach unto thine eyes.

Thisbe

Asleep, my love?

What, dead, my dove?

O Pyramus, arise!

Speak, speak. Quite dumb?

Dead, dead? A tomb
Must cover thy sweet eyes.
These My lips,
This cherry nose,
These yellow cowslip cheeks,
Are gone, are gone:
Lovers, make moan:
His eyes were green as leeks.
O Sisters Three,
Come, come to me,
With hands as pale as milk;
Lay them in gore,
Since you have shore
With shears his thread of silk.
Tongue, not a word:
Come, trusty sword;
Come, blade, my breast imbrue:
Stabs herself
And, farewell, friends;
Thus Thisby ends:
Adieu, adieu, adieu.

From *King Lear*
King Lear

Blow, winds, and crack your cheeks! rage! blow!
You cataracts and hurricanoes, spout
Till you have drench'd our steeples, drown'd the cocks!
You sulphurous and thought-executing fires,
Vaunt-couriers to oak-cleaving thunderbolts,
Singe my white head! And thou, all-shaking thunder,
Smite flat the thick rotundity o' the world!
Crack nature's moulds, an germens spill at once,
That make ingrateful man!

Cordelia

Had you not been their father, these white flakes
Had challenged pity of them. Was this a face
To be opposed against the warring winds?
To stand against the deep dread-bolted thunder?
In the most terrible and nimble stroke
Of quick, cross lightning? to watch—poor perdu!—
With this thin helm? Mine enemy's dog,
Though he had bit me, should have stood that night
Against my fire; and wast thou fain, poor father,
To hovel thee with swine, and rogues forlorn,
In short and musty straw? Alack, alack!
'Tis wonder that thy life and wits at once
Had not concluded all.

GLOSSARY OF THEATER TERMINOLOGY

Action Used in two ways: In a play or scene, the dramatic action is what happens; for an actor, the action is what his or her character does to try to fulfill a need by attaining some objective. Stanislavski spoke of both spiritual (inner) and physical (outer) actions. Note that speaking is one of the most common forms of action; that is, saying is also doing. To be "in action" is to be totally involved in the task at hand and is the most desirable condition for an actor. Action is the most fundamental concept behind most systems of acting. (See also *Automatic action, Choice, Indirect action, Inner action, Justify, Motivation, Objective, Reacting, Score, Stimulus, Strategic choice, Suppression,* and *Verb*.)

Ad lib To insert one's own words into a script, usually on the spur of the moment.

Agent Someone who represents and markets actors. An agent normally gets a 10 percent commission on everything an actor earns. Getting an agent is often the first step in initiating a professional film or television career.

Arc The movement from the low point to the high point of an action; also, the change in a character from the beginning of a play to the end.

Attitude The way a character feels about something that has happened.

Automatic action Stanislavski's term for what we call a habit or reflex; something a character does without thinking.

Backstory Information about a character's life prior to the play, sometimes provided by the playwright but more often created by the actor as part of his or her preparation.

Beat A unit of action with its own specific conflict and crisis. In each beat a character has a single objective. Beats are formed of interactions and flow to create the underlying structure of a scene. The flow of the beats is the primary rhythm of a scene.

Beat change The point at which a character changes a strategy or objective, moving the scene in a new direction.

Believability Consistency with the created reality and style of the world of the story and the personality of the character, whether like everyday life or not.

Bio (See *Résumé*.)

Blocking Establishing the positions and movements of the actors on the stage or in relation to the camera. Good blocking should express the underlying action of the scene.

Breakdown (See *Scenario*.)

Breath cadence (See *Cadences*.)

Cadences The levels of rhythm built into the dialogue; the flow of accented and unaccented syllables, breath phrases, and the length of speeches that form the dialogue.

Call The time an actor is to report for work. Missing a call is a serious offense.

Callback There are usually preliminary auditions in the audition process, from which a small number of actors are called back for a final audition.

Casting director Preliminary auditions, especially in film and television, are usually conducted by a casting director who then selects the actors for callbacks with the director or producer. Casting directors are extremely important to actors starting out; they can be more important to the establishment of a career than are agents.

Centeredness Although it has a literal, physical dimension, being centered implies a unified sense of self that allows actions to involve the whole body and be well focused.

Cheating out Standing so that one's face is turned slightly toward the audience.

Choice When pursuing a need, a character may consider several alternative courses of action and then make a strategic choice that appears to hold out the best chance of success. Examining a character's significant choices can provide a wealth of information about the character.

Climax The "main event," which is the resolution of the underlying conflict of a story and therefore the end of the suspense. Scenes normally do not have climaxes, because the suspense of the story must carry into the next scene.

Conflict The opposition between two forces that underlies a dramatic situation and forces a movement toward resolution. Conflict can be seen on many levels— within a beat, a scene, or the entire play; between characters; or within a character.

Connotation The implications or references of a word at the time the play was written; may be different from the literal dictionary meaning, which is denotation.

Costume parade The first showing of the costumes on the set and under lights for approval by the director.

Craft The body of skills and techniques applied by an effective actor; in German, literally means "power."

Creative state The condition of relaxed playfulness that some psychologists say allows for maximum creativity, when a person's inner parent allows the inner child to come out and play.

Crisis The event in a story after which the outcome becomes, in hindsight, inevitable. Before this point, the energy of the story rises in suspense; during the crisis, the outcome hangs in the balance; and after the crisis, the energy flows toward resolution. Although a crisis (or turning point) leads to a climax, it is not always the same thing as the climax and is often not the emotional high point of a story. A scene has a crisis in which the main issue of that scene is decided. A beat also has a crisis just before the beat change.

Cross An actor's movement from point A to point B. Such movements need to be justified by some inner need. There are different kinds of crosses, such as the banana, which is a slight curve so that the actor ends up cheated out.

Cue Anything that causes something else to happen. For an actor it refers to the line or event just before his or her character speaks or moves. It can also refer to a change in lighting or sound.

Cueing The way in which one line follows another. In real life we often overlap one another in speech and begin responding slightly before the other person has finished speaking. In film, overlapping is sometimes avoided because it limits the editor's ability to cut from take to take. Cueing also means helping actors learn or remember lines by prompting them.

Cue-to-cue A form of technical rehearsal in which the actors are asked to jump from light cue to light cue.

Deliberation The phase of inner action when various possible choices are considered in reaction to a stimulus.

Demonstration Bertolt Brecht's idea that the actor does not become the character completely, but rather demonstrates the character's behavior for the audience while still expressing some attitude about it.

Denotation The literal dictionary meaning of a word at the time the play was written or at the time in which the action is set.

Denouement French for "unraveling"; that final portion of a story in which the loose ends are wrapped up.

Deputy In an Equity company, a member of the cast elected to serve as the representative of the actors to the management. (See also *Equity*.)

Dialogue cadence (See *Cadences*.)

Downstage At one time, stages were sloped to enhance the illusion of perspective, so actors were literally moving "down" stage when heading toward the audience, and they were literally moving "up" stage when backing away from the audience. Even though our stages today are rarely sloped (or "raked"), we still use this terminology.

Dramatic When the outcome of an event is important and cannot be foretold, we say it is dramatic. (See also *Suspense*.)

Dramatic function The job a character was created to do within a story. It can be related to plot, meaning, an understanding of the main character, or any combination of these.

Dress rehearsal The final rehearsals that are conducted under performance conditions.

Dual consciousness An actor's ability to be immersed in a character and the character's world, while still reserving a level of awareness for artistic judgment. Different types of material make different demands on actors; film requires the virtual elimination of the actor's awareness in favor of the character's awareness.

Economy Doing enough to fulfill the dramatic function and believability of a character but avoiding extraneous details or effort.

Emotion memory (or recall) An actor's application of a memory from his or her real or imaginary past to enrich his or her response to the situation in the scene. While this device may be useful in rehearsal, it should never be used in performance for fear of taking the actor out of the here and now.

Empathy An actor's ability to put himself or herself in the place of another person, both for purposes of observation and for applying the Magic If to a role. It is possible to empathize with someone without sympathizing with that person.

Equity The Actors Equity Association (AEA), the main theatrical union for actors. *The Equity Rule Book* establishes the conditions under which actors may work in the theater.

Exposition Information about what has already happened that helps an audience understand what is going on in a story or scene. The difficulty in playing exposition is in not falling into an informational tone. A character must have a reason for providing expository information, and it must be justified by inner need.

Extra A nonspeaking actor who rounds out the reality of a scene.

Focus Whatever an actor is concentrating on at any given moment, usually the character's objective.

Functional traits Those qualities that a character was given (or that an actor provides) to allow the character to believably fulfill his or her dramatic function in the story.

Givens More completely, the given circumstances; the world and situation within which a character lives, especially as the conditions affect his or her action. The circumstances include who, when, and where.

Going up Forgetting lines. Although a terrible experience, forgetting lines can sometimes provide wonderfully rich moments if the actor keeps the action going, perhaps even resorting to paraphrase.

Head shot The glossy 8 × 10 photograph an actor hands out along with his or her résumé. The photograph should be attractive but not limiting in the way it portrays him or her—its function is merely to help someone remember the actor.

Immediacy   The quality of an action or performance that makes it seem to be happening right now, before our eyes, as if for the first time.

Improvisation   Performing without a script. Although most comedic improvs are based on a scenario in which the actors have some idea of the basic beats of the scene and the climax, an open-ended improv may be based on only a situation or a relationship. In traditional theater, some directors use improvisation as a rehearsal device in which the actors explore their characters in situations beyond those contained in the script.

In (or out)   On stage, a turn toward center (or away from center).

In action   (See *Action.*)

Indicating   Showing instead of doing; that is, standing outside the reality of a character and playing the emotion or some quality of the character instead of being immersed in the experience of the action.

Indirect action   When some obstacle, internal or external, impedes direct action, a character may choose an indirect strategy, saying or doing one thing while really intending another. When there is indirect action, there is also subtext. (See also *Subtext.*)

Inner action   The inner process of reaction, attitude, need, and choice that results in outer or observable action. A believable performance integrates inner and outer actions into one flow of stimulus and response. This integration is called justifying the external action by connecting it to an internal process.

Inner monologue   The stream of consciousness of the character. As a training or rehearsal device, actors sometimes verbalize or at least think through their characters' inner monologues to be sure they have provided full inner justification for their external actions.

Intention   (See *Objective.*)

Interaction   One instance of give-and-take between characters, sometimes also called a moment. The validity of each interaction can be judged by asking two questions: First, has one character truly affected the other? Second, does this link in the chain of action and reaction move the scene in the proper direction?

Justification   To connect outer (visible or audible) actions to inner needs and processes. A script provides the basis for outer actions; however much the script may hint at the inner actions that produce the outer actions, it is ultimately the task of the actors to justify the actions. In justifying, the actors put their personal stamp on the performance.

The League of Resident Theatres (LORT)   An organization that has negotiated a specific contract with Actors Equity governing the operation of regional theaters that maintain a resident company. Being a member of a resident company, including performing in the various summer festivals, is the best growth experience an actor can have and is the traditional stepping-stone from training to a professional career.

Magic If   Stanislavski's technique in which actors put themselves in the given circumstances of their characters as if they lived in that world, then experience their characters' needs as if they were their own, and finally choose and pursue their characters' actions as if they were their own. This process results in metamorphosis or transformation, whereby the actor becomes the character, though without losing the dual consciousness that provides artistic control. (See also *Transformation.*)

Metamorphosis   (See *Transformation.*)

Moment   A brief period of time when something of special value is happening. We speak of "making the moment." It can also refer to an interaction between characters; several interactions make up a beat.

Motivation   The inner need that drives a character's action; it usually comes from something that has just happened in a scene, although the need may be long standing. It is important that the energy coming from a past motivation drives the character toward some objective in the immediate future because an actor can't play motivation. Motivation must lead to aspiration.

Need   Something a character lacks or wants that drives him or her to pursue an action to satisfy that lack or desire.

Objective   The goal a character pursues through action to satisfy a need. An objective is best identified using a transitive verb phrase, such as "to persuade him to give me a territory in town." In practice, the most useful form of an objective is a change in the other character, such as "to get him to look at me with compassion"; this draws the actor's energy outward and into the immediate future, bringing him or her into strong interaction with the other character. The terms *intention* and *task* are sometimes used to mean *objective*.

Off book   Performed without the script; that is, with lines memorized. Immediately after going off book, it is expected that an actor will need prompting; he or she should call for lines without apology so that there is no loss of concentration or sense of action.

Pace   The momentum or flow of a scene. Pace is different from tempo, which refers to the speed of the action. Regardless of tempo, a scene has good pace when the connections of cause and effect, action and reaction are strong and real so that the action flows with integrity and purpose. Paradoxically, sometimes slowing the tempo of a scene improves the pace because the actors are forced to experience the connections of action and reaction more fully.

Paraphrase   To use one's own words in place of the words of the script, although with an effort to mean the same thing.

Paraphrasing can sometimes help actors to examine the meaning of their lines and to "own" or personalize them. It can also help carry actors over moments in which they "go up" on their lines.

Personalization   The indispensable process of making a character's needs, choices, habits, and actions one's own. (See also *Magic If.*)

Playable   Referring to an objective or action that is useful in performance and contributes to the movement of the scene. The most playable objectives are SIP: singular, immediate, and personally important.

Play through   Let the action flow with good pace by keeping awareness moving toward a future objective and avoiding falling into internal feelings or the past. An actor's energy is most useful to a scene when it is oriented outward and toward the future.

Plot   The sequence of events as the story unfolds. An actor needs to be aware of how each of his or her actions moves the plot forward, especially when a scene contains a plot point that must be solidly established.

Projection   In the theater, speaking loudly enough and with enough clarity to be heard and understood throughout the auditorium. Good projection is usually more a matter of clarity than of sheer volume.

Prompt book   The copy of the script kept by the stage manager; it contains the blocking, the lighting and sound cues, and all the rest of the physical aspects of a production. It is possible to re-create a production from the prompt book, as is sometimes done in the case of great European productions. Some of Shakespeare's plays were printed from his prompt books.

Prompting   Giving actors lines when they ask for them. Actors usually call out, "Line." Lines are given by the stage manager in a theater and by the script supervisor in film.

Prop   Anything a character handles. It is wise to begin working with rehearsal substitutes as soon as actors are off book.

Psychological gesture   A technique developed by Russian director and teacher Michael Chekhov whereby the actor develops a single physical gesture that triggers a total immersion into the life of the character.

Public solitude   Stanislavski's concept of how actors, by focusing on their objectives, can "forget" that they are in public and thereby avoid self-consciousness and stage fright. The concept does not imply that actors neglect the discipline of producing a publicly effective performance.

Raising the stakes   Heightening the drama of an action or scene by making it more significant or urgent.

Reacting   Responding to an immediate stimulus in a scene; allowing that stimulus to make the actor do whatever his or her character would do in response. This requires real hearing and seeing and the courage to accept the stimulus as the other actor actually provides it, rather than playing what was previously imagined. Because everything a character does is in reaction to something, we say that acting is reacting. The ideal is to be more moved than moving.

Read-through   A rehearsal in which an entire scene or script is read aloud.

Recognition   In Aristotle's sense, the realization of something by a character, usually something of great consequence.

Recognition traits   Qualities given a character to "round them out" as a real human being.

Relationship   All characters exist in relationship to other characters, and we come to understand characters mostly by observing the way others relate to them. For this reason, we say that actors create each other's characters more than they create their own. It is important to develop a character in specific relationship to the performances of the other actors in a scene.

Relaxation   The key to almost everything in acting. For an actor, relaxation is not a reduction of energy but rather a freeing of energy and a readiness to react. The term "restful alertness" is the best description.

Repertory   A company of actors that performs a body of plays. When a number of plays are performed on alternating days, it is called rotating, or true, repertory. The regional repertory movement in this country is an important source of entry-level jobs for young actors.

Résumé   A listing of an actor's experience, showing the roles he or she has performed, including where and under whose direction, as well as training and special skills.

Roback Voco-Sensory Theory   The theory that our language was formed partly by the meaning given to certain sounds by the physical act of pronouncing them.

Running lines   Two or more actors going over their lines together; the best way to memorize lines.

Scale   The "size" of a performance, determined by the demands of the performance environment, from tiny (for film) to huge (for a large auditorium). Whatever the scale, it must be justified by adjustments within the inner phase of the action.

Scenario   A listing of the beats of a scene; also called a breakdown. A scenario gives the actors a sense of the underlying structure of the scene; it serves as a sort of map as they move through the journey of the scene.

Scene   A section of a play that has its own main conflict and crisis. A scene usually contains one of the major events of the story and makes a major change in the plot or central relationship. In some older plays, scenes are marked by the entrance of major characters; these are called "French scenes."

Score   Stanislavski spoke of the score of a role as the sequence of objectives. An actor comes to understand the logic of this sequence, and eventually this flow of action carries him or her through the role, serving as a kind of total choreography for mind and body. (See also *Spine*.)

Sense memory (or recall)   A memory from an actor's real or imagined past of sensations similar to those required by a scene, which can enrich the actor's response to the scene. Stanislavski believed that every cell in the body is capable of such memory and urged actors to develop their storehouse of such memories.

Set up   To prepare for the punch line of a joke, the entrance of a character, or some other important event.

Sides   Sides were small versions of a play that contained only the speeches of individual characters; these are rarely used now.

Spine   Stanislavski spoke of each beat and scene in a role fitting together like the vertebrae in a spine. When an actor experiences this connectedness, the role begins to flow as if under its own power. Also called the through-line of the role; similar to the score of the role, in which the through-line is understood as a sequence of objectives.

Spiritual action   Stanislavski's term for the inner phase of action, which produces physical or external action.

Spontaneity   Each moment of a performance should feel as if it were happening for the first time and yet be controllable and consistent from performance to performance. Stanislavski believed that this could be achieved by rehearsing an act so fully that it becomes "automatic and therefore free"; that is, if an actor doesn't need to think about it, he or she is free to experience it afresh each time it's done.

Stage directions   The indications in a script about a character's gestures, tone of voice, and so on, such as "(*He moves away angrily*)." Some teachers and directors tell actors to ignore stage directions because in some so-called acting versions of a play, the stage directions may have been inserted not by the writer but from the prompt book of an earlier production. However, many writers do provide stage directions, and actors should consider them for the information they contain about the behavior and emotion of their characters, even if that behavior eventually takes a different form in a particular production.

Stage fright   Everyone gets it. The only antidote is to be fully focused on the task at hand and passionately committed to it.

Stage right (or left)   Directions on a stage are given from the actor's point of view as he or she faces the audience; that is, stage right is audience left. In film, the director says either "Move to your right" or "Move to camera left."

Stichomythia   Short, rapid alternation of speeches within the dialogue; used as a special device in classical Greek drama.

Stimulus   What a character is reacting to at any given moment. The most useful stimuli are in the immediate present, however much they may trigger needs or feelings from the character's past.

Strategic choice   A character's sense of how best to pursue an objective within the given circumstances. The strategic choices a character makes express the way he or she sees the world and the other characters.

Substitution   A special kind of emotion recall in which someone from an actor's real or imaginary past is substituted (in the actor's mind) for another character in a scene, to enrich the actor's response to that character. This is a dangerous device because it may take the actor out of the here and now, but with caution it may be useful.

Subtext   When pursuing an objective indirectly, a character may be saying or doing one thing while really meaning another. In such cases there is a difference between the surface activity (the text) and the hidden agenda (the subtext). The character may be conscious or unconscious of the subtext; in either case it is important that the actor avoid bringing the subtext to the surface of the scene by trying to play or indicate it.

Super-choice   The main choice made by a character in a play; this choice will affect the character's life and also reflects his or her superobjective.

Superobjective   A character's main desire in life; a life goal toward which each of his or her objectives is directed. Characters, like people in everyday life, are often unconscious of their life goals, but they pervade everything the characters do.

Suppression   A choice *not* to act in response to a stimulus, but rather to "hold down" the energy the stimulus has aroused. By allowing himself or herself to feel the urge to act and then making the effort to suppress it, an actor can turn a "not doing" into a playable action. A "not doing" is useful because it helps to build suspense.

Suspense   A condition in which something is about to happen but the outcome is delayed and in doubt. The more important the potential event, the more doubtful the outcome, and the longer it is delayed, the greater the suspense. It prompts the question, "What will happen?"

Syllable cadence   (See *Cadences.*)

Table reading   Usually the first rehearsal of a script, in which the actors sit at a table and read it aloud. During any reading, it is important that the actors try to play in relationship and experience the action of the scene, not falling into a flat, "literary" tone.

Task   (See *Objective.*)

Technical rehearsal   In theater, the rehearsal in which the lighting, sound, and nearly completed set are first brought together under the command of the stage manager. At the technical rehearsal, the lighting and sound board operators have their first chance to rehearse their cues, and the designers are seeing the set and props in action. Great patience is required of the actors at a tech rehearsal, which is sometimes quite lengthy.

Tempo   The speed at which a scene is played; not to be confused with pace. An actor must be able to justify the action at any tempo; Stanislavski would sometimes have actors play a scene at various tempos as a training exercise. Within a given tempo, there are variations that produce rhythm.

Tempo-rhythm   The term used by Stanislavski to refer to the whole issue of overall tempo and the variations in tempo that produce the rhythms within a scene. He believed that the tempo-rhythms of a scene are fundamental to the correctness of the action of the scene and "all by themselves" can move an actor to the correct emotion.

Through-line   (See *Spine.*)

Transaction   (See *Interaction.*)

Transformation   The process by which an actor begins to become the character or, more accurately, make the character his or her own. To use the language of William James, the character becomes a new "me" to be inhabited by the actor's "I." Stanislavski used the term "metamorphosis."

Universal   The quality of an action, event, or character trait that allows others to recognize and respond to it as related to their own lives.

Upstage   (See *Downstage.*)

Upstaging   In theater, the positioning of one actor upstage of another so that the downstage actor is forced to turn toward the upstage actor (and away from the audience) to speak. In film or theater, this term also refers to any behavior that draws attention to one actor and away from another; to be avoided.

Verb   The word phrase that succinctly describes an actor's action at a given moment, such as "to persuade." Only transitive verbs are used, and all forms of the verb "to be" (such as "being angry" or "being a victim") are avoided.

Visualization   An actor's ability to imagine a situation, to "see" it in the mind's eye.

Visuo-motor behavior rehearsal (VMBR) A special and effective form of rehearsal that allows an actor to visualize his or her performance under performance conditions while in a relaxed state, allowing his or her deep muscles to respond to the mental image.

INDEX